DATE DUE

Young Children Learning

Young Children Learning

Senses and Sensitivity

Alice Yardley

Principal Lecturer in Education,
Nottingham College of Education

Citation Press · New York · 1973

Published by Evans Brothers Limited
Montague House, Russell Square, London, W.C.1

Citation Press, Library and Trade Division, Scholastic Magazines, Inc.
50 West 44th St., New York, New York 10036

The following are the four titles in the
YOUNG CHILDREN LEARNING series by Alice Yardley:

REACHING OUT

EXPLORATION AND LANGUAGE

DISCOVERING THE PHYSICAL WORLD

SENSES AND SENSITIVITY

Also by Alice Yardley:

THE TEACHER OF YOUNG CHILDREN

YOUNG CHILDREN THINKING

Library of Congress Catalog Card Number: 72-95335
Standard Book Number: 590-07329-x

Cover photograph : Henry Grant, AIIP

Printed in Great Britain by T. and A. Constable Ltd.,
Hopetoun Street, Edinburgh.

PRA 3172

Contents

5

Introduction

The value of education is assessed by its results, and a considerable amount of time and energy is devoted to measuring the child's achievements. A battery of tests and examinations estimates with clinical precision the degree of skill or the quality of intellect attained by the child as a result of our educational system. This is right and reasonable, but is it enough?

Many teachers are aware that the most precise tests can measure only certain qualities, and that at present much the child accomplishes is not measurable. Psychometric tests may classify him as virtually an 'also-ran' when he is, in fact, capable of leading a highly successful life.

The danger lies not in the system but in the attitudes to education engendered by it. Because a measure is there, some adults look only for those qualities in the child that can be measured. Yet each of those adults may be well aware that in his own life there are other and more subtle measures of self-fulfilment. Success in a chosen field may provide him with a comfortable mode of living, or recognition of scholastic achievement may bring with it a fleeting elation, but deep and permanent satisfaction with living is rooted in personality and in those indefinable qualities which are so difficult to assess.

There is a tendency, too, to think that what can't be

measured can't be developed by education. It is assumed that either the child is sensitive, friendly, creative and responsive, or he is not; and yet our observation of children shows us that this is not the whole truth.

If education is to be of service to the individual it must offer him opportunities for growth in every aspect of his person. It must be concerned as much with the language of feeling as with knowledge and skills. A well-informed mind is of no use, either to its owner or to society, unless its contents can be liberated, and this education in communication should range over many diverse fields.

In this book we shall consider the growth and communication of those personal qualities which provide life with its other dimension, which make the difference between living in a dull, flat, two-dimensional way and living as a complete, full and whole human being. Those who can stand aside and scrutinise the aims and procedures of the present-day system are bound to ask, sooner or later, 'Have we got our priorities right?' Only an education which touches the whole of personality is good enough for the children with whom we are entrusted.

It is in this book, on *Senses and Sensitivity*, that I have felt at liberty to express some of my deepest beliefs about the nature of education and to record many profound experiences which have enriched my life as a person. I have grown increasingly aware that helping children to become all that they are capable of becoming is a way of life rather than merely a vocation which provides a means of living. With Sir Herbert Read (in *Education through Art*) I recognise too that the teacher 'learns his responsibility for the particle of life entrusted to his care, and as he learns he educates himself . . . The education of a pupil is thus always the self-education of the teacher'.

Acknowledgements

I am indebted throughout to Allen Young who, with infinite patience, read and checked the manuscript. In those aspects of the work which are associated with music, the advice of my colleague Malcolm Anderton has proved invaluable. Malcolm Anderton also compiled the list of suggestions for music suitable for use with young children. The ideas expressed in Chapter 9, 'The foundation of belief', owe much to the inspiration of my colleague Robin Protheroe. He also supplied the list of books offering guidance to teachers who are anxious to help young children develop soundly-based religious concepts.

1

The foundation of learning

As educators, parents and teachers must stand aside from time to time and ask, 'What do we want for our children? What do we hope to do for them? What do we feel they should become?'

Many adults in our society still think of education in terms of intellectual development and see the work of the schools as preparation for achievement in examinations, leading to a career. There is, perhaps, some recognition of the fact that as human beings we feel, and that somewhere along the line the education of feeling offers a little light relief from the chores of learning. When facts and procedures, memorised for examination purposes, have been forgotten, the final product of education is the sort of person that is left. Those experiences which have enlarged the person are as enduring as personality itself, and the enrichment of vital personal experience is what education is about.

If the emphasis in educational practice is preponderantly intellectual, the outcome can only be intellectual aridity. The full development of balanced, whole persons leads to enrichment in every aspect of the person; and the education of feeling doesn't just happen, it needs as much attention as any other form of development. If we hope for the child above all to have an adequate intellectual adjustment to his world, then we must educate him to feel as well as to think. The intellect is fed by experience. We can merely pass through experience or we can be fully aware of it, and a conscious awareness of the world depends on the quality of our personal response to it.

However, many people who are influential in educational affairs do not recognise the importance of feeling. In some, deep personal feeling has never really awakened, and they plan for children along the lines of their own limited education. They may even feel a sense of resentment towards the person who can honestly enjoy his feelings, and a genuine display of feeling may be embarrassing to them or slightly indecent – something to be 'brought under control' or 'stamped out'.

Some make a conscious show of putting aesthetic education on the programme and treating it as a subject, to be kept tidily in a compartment. Education for such people is seen in terms of subjects and skills. They think of personality as some separate part of the child which fits in alongside the things he learns. Such people keep feeling at a distance, allowing it to be indulged in occasionally but not to be considered as of intrinsic value to education.

The other three books of this series considered the nature of learning and the development of the child as an individual. Practically all that a person achieves must be learned; learning starts at birth, and, urged on by an exploratory drive, the human baby strives to make sense of his world and to adjust to it. Knowledge of his surroundings depends on his capacity to obtain information about them. The quality of learning is closely related to the amount of personal effort made on the part of the individual, and learning at first hand through one's own resources is far more effective than learning through being told. These resources are the sense organs and the capacity to respond emotionally. The human baby has much to learn and the process covers the whole of a lifetime, the most active part of it taking place in the first quarter of that life, from birth to the age of maturity.

None of the child's achievements are accomplished in isolation. Learning to speak is linked with the need to communicate, with experiences and feelings which give rise to communication, with the thoughts and ideas which provide speech with meaning, and with the physical use of the organs of speech. These things cannot be learned one at a time, and what affects a single aspect of the activity affects the whole activity; poor hearing, a hare-lip, limited experiences, emotional apathy can each affect speech as powerfully as can intellectual dullness itself.

We give full recognition to the effects of innate ability on the child's capacity to learn, and we know that as the child's individual pattern of learning develops, his various aptitudes emerge. We know too that there is much we can do to bring these aptitudes to life, and that the most powerful form of motivation stems from the child's own purpose. When a child urgently wants to learn his sense of purpose unifies his energies, and all his resources are devoted to the accomplishment of his purpose. Wanting to perform a task will awaken the capacity to attempt it.

Most of us go through life with many of our aptitudes untapped. Perhaps the stimulus came too soon, or too late, to evoke maximum response, and we lacked sufficient personal drive to stir the dormant ability. Indeed very few people reach full potential, but it is never too late in life to discover unexpected depths in oneself if the stimulus is sufficiently vital. A crisis often reveals hidden ability, but most of us fear personal disturbance and try to avoid being put to the test.

Full personal involvement comes naturally to young children. Mark is four. He lives in a new bungalow, and the bungalow next door is in the course of erection. Through a whole morning Mark followed the bricklayer, watching his skilled craftsmanship with absorbed interest. It was difficult for his mother to divert his attention, even to the cup of hot cocoa she prepared for him at eleven o'clock. He asked what the 'porridge stuff' was that went between the bricks and why the bricks

13

weren't piled up without it, but most of the time he sought answers to his questions in observation.

Lunchtime came and the men knocked off. Mark was persuaded to eat his stew and vegetables and then returned to his post. Ten minutes later he had placed the next three bricks along the wall with surprising dexterity, giving each a neat tap with the handle of the trowel to set it into position. The intensity of his interest had sharpened his observation, and only practice and muscular strength were needed to enable him to acquire the skill he emulated.

Mark gave little heed to the passage of time or to the fact that this lesson lasted for nearly three hours. He didn't concern himself with the value to himself of acquiring such a skill. He didn't stop to think of the labour involved in lifting heavy bricks. He was interested and curious. He admired the workman who could perform such a wonderful task, and in his imagination he envisaged himself as the bricklayer. He wanted to perform the same skill and found its performance a joyful accomplishment. On that morning there was nothing else he would rather have done.

How often in adult life do we allow for full personal involvement? How often do we have time to follow our inclinations? Because we want a number of material things from life we enslave ourselves to accomplishing what other people demand of us. We lose the art of being caught up – mind, body and emotions – in what tries to capture our attention, and so we lose the drive of inner direction and accept other direction. We become frustrated, disillusioned, unsatisfied, and leave only time and room for a superficial half-life.

Ultimately what we would want for our children is what we would want for ourselves. We want to extend to each of the children we teach full opportunity to become a whole person, who is capable of living as completely as he is equipped to live. We recognise the unique nature of each child and we want to earn for him the right to be that individual person and nobody else.

It takes a great deal of courage to put what we believe into practice, to have faith in the educative value of materials and in the child's individual way of learning from them. Too often we provide good materials and equipment and then direct the child into using them according to some project of our own. We decide in advance what each child shall do with his materials, what he shall learn from them and how he shall learn it. We have no faith in the child's individual approach to experience, in his ability to learn at first hand from materials and to gain from their intrinsic value. We do not understand the real nature of experience and think of it as merely doing, or being active.

We call our ideas 'topics', 'centres of interest', or 'projects', and we expect the child to express what we have in mind. He produces a model farm, or a seashore, or a fun-fair from material which might fire his imagination in a different direction if only we allowed it. We may give the child the raw materials of the earth itself in the form of clay, but then we allow him no chance to discover the characteristics and idiosyncrasies of his material, nor to build up a relationship with it. We are preventing that act of creation which can be the outcome of a partnership between child and material, that opportunity for something to result from this unique relationship. The result of our demands is a neat little thumb-pot, and what it could have been we shall never know. We may be so concerned with a superficial result that we provide little opportunity for experience in depth.

Our responsibility to children is to give them full experience of the present. We are investing in their future by ensuring for them the opportunity to gain full benefit from the actual and the immediate. By enabling them to exercise their powers of absorption, we provide the opportunity for depth of experience and consequently for depth of feeling. They can then acquire as habits the feeling of being deeply stirred and of living completely. Society needs balanced personalities who know what life is about and how it can be lived before it needs people who can conform to prescribed patterns of efficiency, who are prepared to potter out an existence as a human computer or a mechanical robot.

'An essential part of our job as educators is to help people to achieve depth and sincerity of feeling', says Jeffreys in his book *Personal Values in the Modern World*. 'For it is quite certain that no one can be a public leader who cannot enter into the feelings of the people at large.'

In this book we shall examine the true nature of experience and the means by which the child can learn from it. We shall try to decide what in life is worthwhile, and how we can help the child to become aware of it. We shall consider the significance of complete personality, and of what it means to live in the fullest sense of the word. By so doing we may catch a glimpse here and there of the fundamental purpose of education and of our work as teachers and parents.

2

Sensory and emotional knowledge

Feeling is a term we associate with sensory experience. It also refers to the excitement of the emotions. There is a firm relationship between sensory and emotional aspects of feeling, and much of what the child learns, particularly during his early years, is rooted in this relationship.

From the moment of birth the child is able to respond emotionally. His emotional responses are part of his natural behaviour, and he doesn't need to learn them. During the early weeks of life emotional experience involves the baby in a total excitement of the whole organism; evidence of this state is seen in the way he waves his limbs about, in the changing colour of his skin and in the vocal sounds he makes.

At first emotional response is either generally positive and an expression of satisfaction, contentment and well-being, or generally negative and an expression of discomfort, deprivation and distress. As yet, there is little apparent discrimination between such positive emotional responses as pleasure, satisfaction, joy and happiness, and between such negative responses as pain, aggression, misery and dissatisfaction. An ever-widening range of emotions of both kinds develops along with other powers of differentiation.

Which kinds of emotion predominate in later life depend on the emotional environment provided for the child by adults during his early years. The child brought up in a secure and loving home, where people are favourably disposed towards him, will develop the habit of being generally happy; whereas the child brought up in conflict and discord, surrounded by people who regard him as a burden and a nuisance, will develop a more generally negative response to life.

When children first enter school, their reactions to an unfamiliar social group show immediately the emotional climate of the home. Ian is a friendly, outgoing child, who expects people to like and accept him. Things may go wrong with him from time to time, but the emotional stability of his home has taught him that on the whole the world is a good place to live in, and any ill-feeling he finds in it is only temporary. Donald, on the other hand, is apprehensive. He sees the world as a hostile place, and expects the people in it to treat him unkindly, with only the occasional kindly gesture to lighten the gloom.

The basic attitude to life established in a child before he faces the world outside his family colours the response he gets from other people. When Donald cowers away from his teacher and is prepared to fight the first child to lay a finger on his new shoe-bag, it is difficult to approach him in a warm and friendly way. Ian, who naturally loves everybody on sight and is prepared to find the world an exciting place to share with other people, makes friends quickly and finds that people are always ready to help him.

At home and in school the mental health of the child is an important responsibility of the adult. Young children depend on adults, particularly on those they love and who satisfy their physical needs. They are extremely vulnerable in their dependence, and they need to feel not only accepted but approved of. They need help in learning about their own emotions and how to handle them. They need to find emotional stability, and to have the support of an adult who is mature enough to deal with the difficult situations which arise from immature

18

emotional behaviour. The adult who can accept as normal a very wide range of behaviour and remain serenely unmoved by it, provides a refuge for the child and a source of healing when emotions make a battlefield of his personality. Serenity in a responsible adult has a more salubrious mental effect on the child than any other single factor in his environment.

Dave is five. His parents were separated and it was Grandma who brought him up while mother functioned as the bread-earner. When Grandma died Dave's life was shattered. He bitterly resented the separation from the one person on whom he could depend for the satisfaction of his physical and emotional needs. In spite of the attention of a kindly aunt who tried to take Grandma's place while his mother was at work, he became almost uncontrollably aggressive. Knowing the home circumstances his teacher remained undisturbed by his behaviour and whenever possible found him jobs which absorbed him and gave him a measure of respite from his own conflicts. Dave was quietened by her presence, and would bring his picture book and settle beside her, turning the pages. Eventually he began to talk about Grandma, and his teacher helped him to make a book about her. He took the book home to show his mother, and this was the beginning of his adjustment to the great upheaval in his life. He became able to accept the loving care of his aunt.

In *Exploration and Language* we saw how the meaning associated with a word originates in the child's sensory and emotional experiences. The young child knows much about warmth, for instance, long before he knows the word for it. He associates the physical sensation of heat with the emotional satisfaction it brings him. When he becomes aware of the word 'warm', and later learns to say it, both sensory and emotional experience will provide the symbol with meaning.

Personal experience is a synthesis of sensory and emotional experience, and out of it thought emerges. As the child acquires words he acquires the means of shaping his thoughts.

Experience, stored in the form of images and words, is the foundation of the child's mind, and the more meaning he attaches to words the greater the quality of his thoughts.

In school we aim to provide the child with a wide range of experiences which are full of feeling, both sensory and emotional, and therefore full of meaning for him. The vocabulary the child acquires will be enriched with the meaning which is built into his person as a result of the things he has done.

When a person experiences something deeply, whether it is through his intellect, his imagination, his senses or his feelings, he has an urge to express it. Man needs a vehicle of expression, a means of communicating his experiences to himself and to other people, for expressing an experience extends and enlarges that experience. It enables man to understand the experience more deeply and to see the effects of it on his personality. He may also need to pass on the experience to another person, and to exchange it with the experiences of others.

However vital thoughts and feelings may be, man cannot transfer them from his mind to the mind of another. He can only pass on information about them, in the hope that the receiver will make something of it. The quality of that information depends on the materials which are used to convey it. Some thoughts may be adequately communicated by means of words, others require the notes of music or a plastic medium such as clay. A wide choice of materials enables man to select those most suitable as a vehicle for his thoughts.

It is in childhood that these powers of communication begin to develop. When we provide children with the opportunity to experience at depth we must also provide a range of materials which will enable them to express the effects of these experiences. This range must be wide enough to allow for adequate experimentation. Children think and feel in different ways, and for each child there are materials which best suit his individual needs. We place at the disposal of children such basic physical materials as sand, clay, wood, stone, soil, water, air and sound, together with man-made fabrics, paints, marking media and fibres, odds and ends of all kinds for making pictures and models. Equally important are abstract materials in the shape of notes, numbers, words and many other of man's symbols. Each child discovers through experimenting that some of these materials are more suitable than others to convey a particular type of experience, and that he wants to adopt for more regular use those materials which best suit his personality. Thus, at the adult stage one person is particularly gifted with words, another with paint or clay, while others find themselves using notes with great skill, or turning to soil or water as their most natural means of expression.

When we give children real materials such as water, sand, clay or sound, their curiosity is so intense that they seem to identify with their materials completely. A child who is allowed to make his own relationship with clay will pummel and knead, poke and flatten and hammer until the material and the child become one, and the visual results are the effects of an experience shared. The child and the stuff in his hands embark on their exploration of one another, and the clay takes on a form which becomes an expression of the feeling which consumed the child as he worked. Feeling and form are two aspects of a single experience, and as a result of this partnership something is created which neither alone could have achieved.

Good provision and a helpful atmosphere will encourage the child to liberate his feelings and to explore ways of expressing them. A teacher can help a child to become more aware of his surroundings and so open up for him the opportunity to perceive at greater depth, but she cannot force a child to feel. Education can help to develop a child's powers of perception and observation, but genuine sensitivity can only develop spontaneously.

Bobby was a difficult child to handle. His home background

stifled sensitivity rather than encouraged it. He seemed unaware of the needs of other children and constantly demanded his teacher's attention. Even when another child was ill he would try to divert attention to himself by some outrageous behaviour such as knocking over the paint jars. His teacher was particularly careful to keep a vigilant eye on Bobby when he was near objects of cultural value, as he was quite capable of tipping water from a vase of flowers over a length of Chinese silk displayed for the enjoyment of the children. Indeed, the only positive response evident in Bobby was in the 'movement' period, and here he found a release for his feelings which took on a form of emotional exposure which was quite terrifying to watch. One day his teacher played the record of the Peer Gynt Suites. Bobby seemed caught up in the ecstasy of the music, which seemed to provide him with a means of expressing his feelings. Other children were drawn into the dance he created, and for the first time he seemed able to share feeling with others. This was the beginning of Bobby's awareness of other children.

Man's use of words as a means of communication is perhaps more highly prized than any other of his gifts. In some schools the emphasis throughout is on verbal modes of expression. Creative materials and exploratory pursuits are regarded as relaxation, while the business of getting the child to use words skilfully is considered to be of paramount importance.

Linguistic skill is highly desirable in a literate society, but it is not achieved by using words to the exclusion of other materials. The child needs to say what he will in as many ways as possible, and each new and unique experience will help to enrich his verbal material. The words he uses depend for their meaning on association with physical experience and the ideas which emerge from it. Becoming articulate is only one facet of becoming a person.

Sarah accompanied her father on a drive over a mountain pass and down a valley. It was a showery day and rainbows echoed one another along the valley. The phenomenon thrilled Sarah, and the following day in school she needed paint to communicate her experience, even before she expressed it in words. In her first pictures she used the full range of rainbow colours to portray her impressions. She then selected green and concentrated on depicting the vivid greens of the grass and trees as she remembered them 'at the end of the rainbow'. Her final picture was entirely green in a hundred different shades. Then she turned to words and beneath her picture she wrote:

> 'When it rains the people say
> I wish it was another day.
> But don't be sad on a rainy day
> When the rain's gone away a rainbow you will find.'

What a person takes from any experience is entirely personal and unique. It remains for ever private and can never be completely conveyed to another, and yet man strives constantly to share what he has with others. By so doing he enriches his private experiences, for the more articulate he becomes about his thoughts and impressions, the greater is his satisfaction in them. When we help children to acquire a wide variety of ways in which to express themselves we help them to deepen each moment of their lives.

In Herbert Read's words, 'The aim of education is (therefore) the creation of artists – of people efficient in the various modes of expression' (*Education through Art*).

3

The child and his materials

Human development is the outcome of continuous interaction between the person and the world surrounding him. The child reaches out to explore and what he finds stimulates further exploration. Personal contact with what the outer world provides leads to internal impressions and responses, and these stimulate communication. There is constant interchange between the world of understanding within the person and the comprehended world without. The link between the two depends on the many materials available to man.

The most versatile and satisfying of all materials are those which are natural to man. Deep in each of us is the primitive urge to manipulate, explore and use for our own purposes the stuff of the earth itself. Soil and sand, stone and wood, water and air and natural objects of all kinds are the materials man first used. They remain as satisfying and educative today as they were in man's earliest days of development. These are the materials the child first needs. No one has to tell him to play with them, or what they are for. The adult simply provides access to them, and the child's curiosity makes him reach out in an attempt to relate them to himself.

Whatever the material may be, the child goes through two distinct stages in his handling of it. The first stage is exploratory. Intense curiosity promotes avid investigation, and the

24

efforts of the child are directed towards finding out what his materials are like, what they will and will not do, and what he can do with them. Tension and effort are characteristic of this stage, and there is often little concern for an end-product. The child concentrates on forcing the material to reveal its true nature. The second stage is a more relaxed and pleasurable experience. Familiarity provides an ease of relationship, in which materials are persuaded to fulfil some purpose for the child.

In school, teachers frequently have the opportunity to introduce the child to unfamiliar materials, such as clay, paint, sand and fabrics, for picture-making. A teacher may feel dismayed when her imaginative collection of materials produces little of apparent artistic value in the early stages of the child's acquaintance with them. The child may handle scraps of fur and velvet with excitement, ruffle the fronds of feathers, or dangle shimmering sequins from a thread of cotton in delighted glee, yet show little inclination to arrange these treasures on paper. Even when he asks for the adhesive, he may say he 'wants to do some sticky' and he may pile all the scraps he most enjoys into a shapeless mass on the paper.

This exploratory behaviour may appear to lead nowhere. In her anxiety to encourage the child to pursue a worthwhile goal, the teacher may outline a shape and suggest to the child that he fills it in with scraps of fabric. Spectacular results can be achieved in this way; but the idea originates in the mind of the teacher, and the child's efforts are being used to express her images. Such results are limiting and may stifle the unique ideas of the child. On the other hand, the teacher who has the courage to allow ample time for exploration is usually rewarded when the child unexpectedly finds in his materials a means of conveying some idea of his own. What the child discovers about his materials must be absorbed by him, or internalised, before he can use materials in a masterly way. Time is an essential factor in the development of relationships between the child and his materials, and the teacher should ensure that the child has time at his disposal.

When children are given creative opportunities the day must be organised to allow for continuous experience – a chance to finish what is attempted, the time to become absorbed and to gain full satisfaction from what is handled. Only by being left face to face with his materials will the child come to know them; the creator and the stuff he is using need to be alone, and direction from without is in conflict with the creative urge. Only when the child and his material become one will the material speak to him, and the imposition of adult ideas will inhibit, or even destroy, creative communication.

When the child is free to come to terms with materials, when he can explore under the guidance of his own curiosity and not in ways directed by the teachers, he will handle his materials in a wide variety of ways which are truly creative. This doesn't mean that the teacher must stand by while precious scraps of silk are wastefully mutilated. The child will appreciate her help in using choice materials with economy, and he will gladly accept the suggestion that a flower the size of a pea should be cut from the corner rather than from the centre of a square foot of expensive felt. What the teacher must do is to resist the temptation to sacrifice the child's educative exploratory experience for the sake of producing results for her own satisfaction.

Too often the teacher's desire for visible results hurries the child through the educative stages of experience. She tells him a story which excites and absorbs him and fires his imagination. When the story is finished, she hands the child a piece of paper and tells him to draw his story, or expects him to play it out in dramatic form. The child must have time to absorb the story, to allow his imagination to recreate it, to respond in many ways and to make the experience part of himself, before he can be expected to express his responses. As Jeffreys says, 'If children are to respond honestly to experience, experience must not be immediately pulled to pieces by the teacher, as one might catch a butterfly and pull its wings off.'

Repeated emphasis on the end-product leads to shallow and inadequate feeling, for it is the exploratory process which educates and which effects a change in personality. Sometimes the growth of the person is the product.

These principles apply to materials of all kinds. They also hold true whether the child approaches materials at the age of two, or ten, or sixteen. Students entering college frequently find themselves confronted with materials they had little opportunity to explore during the years of academic study in a Grammar School. As mature people they may go through the exploratory stages more quickly than young children. Very often, however, they require more time to adjust to new experiences, and learning can be a painful process for the adult who has come to regard clay as dirty stuff which makes a mess of one's finger-nails.

Creative work of quality is encouraged when the child's attitude to his materials is one of positive enjoyment. The way in which he is introduced to them helps to decide his attitude, and the teacher is responsible for helping him to develop positive attitudes towards the things he handles.

When initiating fresh interests the teacher is wisely guided by her own enthusiasm. If she loves wood, or colour, or sounds, or words, this is where she should start. Materials she merely tolerates can come later, when perhaps she has learned to cultivate her pleasure in them through that of the children.

Mrs P. loved poetry. One September day her children asked if they could turn the nature table into a harvest display. Mrs P. started it off by arranging display shelves at four levels. On the top shelf she set a brown pottery jug filled with stalks of corn; then each child brought something which he had grown and grouped his produce on the shelves, forming a fruit shelf, a vegetable shelf, a greenhouse produce shelf, and a herb shelf. They brought masses of flowers too. The lovely fruit reminded Mrs P. of Christina Rossetti's *Goblin Market*, which on impulse she read to the children. They were thrilled by the images and delighted with the words.

The next morning, Mrs P. heard one child say to a little girl who had been absent when the poem was read, 'You should a' been here yesterday, Dian. Miss read us a lovely story poom.' Mrs P. was asked to read the poem again for Dian's benefit. Later on in the day some of the children began to paint, and their wonderful pictures were clearly inspired by the poem. Mrs P. mounted these pictures and wrote parts of the poem underneath them. The children read the poetry to themselves again and again, asking about words they didn't know. Then they quoted sections of the poem, such as:

> 'Figs to fill your mouth,
> Citrons from the South,
> Sweet to tongue and sound to eye;
> Come buy, come buy.'

In her own free writing one child used the phrase 'Sweeter than honey from the rock'. Other children asked Mrs P. to lend them her private anthology so that they could read the poem for themselves, even though they had to struggle with it. Some of the children brought more poems by Christina Rossetti to school. Their interest in poetry was thoroughly awakened, and Mrs P. read to them from Burns, Tennyson and De la Mare. The children loved it and their own writing was vitalised by their increased interest in words.

'I went to church,' wrote Dian, 'all dressed in yellow. I felt lovely and I sparkled like a light.' Mrs P.'s love of poetry had enthused the children, and her own feeling for the words conveyed the meaning to the children.

Miss B. made all her own clothes and revelled in beautiful fabrics. She was particularly sensitive to texture and loved subtle and neutral shades. She saved scraps of many materials and took them to school. Her children listened entranced as she told them the story of silk and of people who made Chinese embroidery, of the protective fur of some animals whose colouring serves as camouflage, of rich velvet and the ceremonial robes made from it, of the homely Irish linen weaves, and hand-made lace and the woven tweeds. She encouraged the children to finger fabrics and to listen to the sounds made by different materials rubbed between their fingers. She left the fabrics for them to enjoy, without demanding that they should 'make something'. She was satisfied that they should share her own simple delight in them.

Some of the children spent a lot of time handling the fabrics and chattering to one another about them. 'Fur is smooth if you stroke it this way, but if you stroke it back again it's a bit rough.' 'This is pure silk and it feels softer than tricel "silk". If I had a lot of silk, I'd wear a beautiful dress with lots of skirts and a velvet cloak that flowed behind when I ran.' 'You can see this linen's made of grass stuff. Its got thick and thin bits in it. My Mum's got an Irish linen table cloth and when she irons it the threads go silky and stiff.' Dave didn't join in this chatter. He sat with a scrap of velvet between his fingers and a faraway look in his eyes.

Some days later, three little girls brought a newspaper cutting about life in India. 'Can we have some of those velvets and silks?' they asked. 'We want to make an Indian market.' Thus, some children approached picture-making through the fabrics themselves, and designs and images grew from their imaginative fingering of the pieces.

Other children wanted to sew the pieces, and they made tiny figures from pipe-cleaners and dressed them. One child gathered all the odd scraps discarded by the other children and sewed them into a patchwork picture. Sue appeared to abandon the fabrics, but she went to the writing corner, made herself a book and wrote about 'Miss B.'s Sewing Pieces'.

Interesting creative work developed in both of these situations because the children were fired by the enthusiasm of their teacher. Attractive and imaginative materials can in themselves inspire some children, but many of our children need help from their teacher if they are to become thoroughly awakened to the qualities of the materials we offer them. When the teacher herself has fingers which feel instead of merely touching, eyes which observe instead of merely seeing, and ears which listen instead of merely hearing, she has the power to sensitise the children she teaches, and to help them to develop that sense of awareness which adds a new dimension to everything they do. It is in this way that materials become a source of creative thought.

4

The educative value of basic materials

Every material has a discipline of its own and in itself has much to teach the child. What, for instance, can we discover about such simple basic materials as clay and wood?

We get to know about clay by handling it, and what we do with it depends on a sense of form, for it offers little in the way of colour and demands of us that we treat it in a solid, three-dimensional way. When clay is in good condition it is extremely plastic and responsive. The touch of a finger leaves an impression and it tempts the hands to squeeze, smooth, pummel, poke and shape. A child of two may find clay a difficult material, because his hands are small and his muscles lack strength enough to master it. But by the time the child is three or four he can handle a lump large enough to be used; his hands can go right round it, and the message of its wholeness is conveyed to him.

Because clay responds readily and impressions are immediate, it is a very personal material and a child using it becomes readily absorbed. It inspires the child to create and to express himself. At the same time it demands of him that it should be used in a special way, for it presents him with a number of problems and challenges him into accepting its discipline. He must learn how to mould an arm for his man from the clay with which he makes the body, because an arm stuck on later will fall off as it dries out. Clay dries fairly quickly and

31

crumbles easily if it isn't moist enough; on the other hand its surface can be etched and textured. It can be smoothed by stroking it with water; in a firm condition it can be carved or engraved. There are many ways in which it can be handled, and success in the use of it depends on its condition.

Comparing clay with a plastic material such as plasticine reveals the limitations of man-made materials. By comparison plasticine is easy. It requires little skill in handling, poses fewer problems and offers fewer rewards. Its use is incidental for instance as a base on which to stand a tree or fence, and it has little creative or educative value.

Information about clay as a natural material will help the child to use it to greater effect. It is derived from rotten granite and is often found quite near the surface. Clay must be kneaded thoroughly to drive out air bubbles. It should be stored in a cool place and covered with a damp sack. It need take up little room in storing as it prefers to be kept out of doors. In a pottery workers pulverise hard clay to a powder, which is placed in a trough; a bucket of water is added, and it is then covered and left for twenty-four hours, at which stage it is ready to knead. Firing clay makes it watertight and durable. Pots have been made from clay for thousands of years.

Sometimes in schools we find clay used to simulate objects. We find clay boats, flowers, even clay igloos. Should we degrade clay in this way? Should we paint clay? Should we varnish it? Or should we encourage its use as a creative medium in its own right?

Wood is another natural material which can be handled in a wide variety of ways. It differs fundamentally from clay in that fingers make little impression on it and tools are essential for effective handling of it. But wood is not used in schools as widely as it should be; many women teachers avoid woodwork because it involves a certain amount of noise or because they themselves dislike handling tools. Wood is expensive and very often children are given the wood from orange boxes and packing cases. This is very difficult material indeed and is not suitable for beginners.

Wood can be treated as a solid medium and carved or sculptured, or it can be used in strips and pieces for construction. A love and respect for wood will develop in children if they are encouraged to discover its characteristics and to learn something about its origins, starting with the trees which grow in the neighbouring environment. Bark, twigs and seeds from the trees can be used in picture-making, and all of this helps the child to build up a knowledge of his material.

Introducing a wide range of wood samples to children can inspire them to use the material imaginatively. Simply through handling different kinds of wood they will discover that it varies in hardness and weight, that it can be polished until it acquires the sheen of silk, that the delicate flower of its grain enhances each piece with a swirling pattern. Most wood floats, although ebony sinks, and some woods float higher in the water than others. It is easy to see why Balsa wood is used for rafts. Wood varies in colour, and the colour and grain become part of what is created from it; the artist carves with these qualities in mind. Wood burns and the charcoal which remains can form part of the child's creative work.

Planing wood produces shavings of many interesting shapes, and sawing it produces sawdust which itself can be used as a creative medium, particularly when mixed with thin glue. Tools play an important part in the use of wood. The five-year-old appreciates a light hammer, a hack-saw, a screwdriver and a vice to hold his wood firm. The seven-year-old enjoys using a drill to provide purchase for his screws and a claw hammer to prise out nails. A file and some sandpaper help a child to produce a more finished job. Such simple equipment is safe for the beginner to use, and in fact the child rarely has accidents with such tools. He isn't afraid of using them, and he handles them with confidence. It is his teacher who is more likely than he to handle them clumsily.

A strong adhesive helps to keep wood in place. We no longer need to employ the dangerous glue-pot, for synthetic adhesives such as Gluak and E.V.C. are strong enough to serve the child's purpose. The addition of ready-turned wheels and strips of dowelling rod will add imaginative dimensions to model-making. A firm box, barrel, or bench to work on completes the equipment.

When children first use materials such as wood, they want to accomplish their task quickly. As they become more ambitious, they encounter more difficult problems and learn that patience and time are essential to good craftsmanship. There is a world of difference between the two slats nailed at right-angles which form the five-year-old's aeroplane, and the complicated model with wheels that satisfies the seven-year-old. Colouring for the five-year-old means using the same powder paint he applies to paper. The seven-year-old needs enamel and finds that wood must first be smoothed in order to achieve a good finish.

We could examine the child's approach to many materials, and we would find that his responses vary little. Once he has made some initial discoveries about the characteristics and behaviour of his material, he starts to use it creatively as a medium for expression. He is rarely interested in learning how to use it apart from making the things he wants.

The question of teaching techniques arises. Do we teach the child how to use tools and materials in prescribed ways, and if we do, when do we teach him? Techniques have little educative value in themselves and should never be introduced before the urge to create has given the child a purpose in using a material. Techniques are a matter of building up a good relationship between the creator and his material. They are personal, but they frequently assume a common pattern because a particular way of doing a job is the most economical and effective. When left to make their own relationships with tools and materials, many children develop their own ways of dealing with them. A vigilant and skilful craftsman can encourage the more effective usage and from time to time suggest, or demonstrate, an appropriate technique.

Each child needs help in selecting the material which best suits his purpose. If there is a wide variety available, the child will discover that the fairy figures of his imagination are better fashioned from paper than clay, and that clay makes a more solid-looking mountain than cardboard ever could. The artist selects his materials with great care, knowing that what he has to say is expressed partly in the material he uses.

The teacher is responsible for ensuring that the materials and tools available suit the stage reached by the child. For instance, she offers the five-year-old beginner powder paint to mix with water, or ready-mixed poster paint. As he gains skill with the use of a brush she adds a wider range of paints, oil-paints, enamel and materials such as paste, sawdust, crushed egg-shell and so on, to add texture and interest to his paint. In this way she helps the child to gain experiences which enable him to discriminate between materials and the ways of using them. He will make fewer mistakes if his experience is varied, and if he has met his materials only when he is able to handle them.

An excellent source of creative materials is the out-of-doors environment, and many of these cost nothing at all. Dried moss, dead leaves, grass, stalks, feathers, bark, sheep's wool, teasels, seeds, twigs, straw, hay – there is an unlimited supply of imaginative materials for picture-making. These various raw materials can inspire children who may find in the more traditional materials less to stimulate them. In some places native materials have been used for local crafts. Wattles and reeds are used to make baskets, fibres give rise to the linen industry, wool to spinning, weaving and dyeing, and so on. Part of the child's exploration of his environment is the study of these local crafts. Vital interests of this kind provide starting points for studies which may lead in many directions.

In one area the local clay was used for making bricks and flower-pots. Some children visited the brickyard with their teacher, where they saw the kilns and many thousands of bricks stacked ready for despatch. Later, attempts to make their own bricks and then to use them for building purposes led to a study of construction, from tunnels and bridges to walls and houses. Brick pavements were found in a local park, and the children discovered that there were many kinds of bricks serving different purposes.

Some of the humble materials used in the classroom have educative value too. Each kind of paste has its own discipline. Paper clips and fasteners, drawing pins, string, cotton, chalk, gummed stars and indeed all the trivia of the classroom have something to teach the child, but their value to him is greater when he is allowed to find out by experiment what they can do, and what he can and cannot do with them. Show him the correct way to use a paper fastener and he may never adventure beyond that way of using it. Left to his imagination, the paper fastener will serve as eyes, or jewels, or tiny dolls, to meet his need.

The materials we have considered so far have been of a concrete and tangible nature. Do the same principles apply to abstract materials such as words and numbers, notes and symbols of every kind? Many teachers who would willingly leave the child free to learn directly from clay and wood, water and sand, paint and fabrics, might question his ability to learn directly from the symbols he finds in his environment. Because symbols are abstract many teachers feel insecure unless they tell children what they are and how to use them. A teacher may feel able to allow the child to explore musical sound and rhythm, even maps and diagrams; but when she is confronted with words and numbers she may cling to the idea that only the adult is capable of understanding them, and that children can only learn about them by being told. Where children have been given opportunities to acquaint themselves freely with words and numbers and other symbols, their original and individual use of them has produced unexpected and imaginative results of outstanding quality. (Many examples have already been quoted, particularly in *Exploration and Language* in this series.) Teachers frequently find that when children have access to many forms of self-expression, the quality of their creative use of symbols is vastly improved.

When using concrete materials the child produces visible evidence of his personality. He discovers much about himself as he tussles with wood and nails, or uses words as an outlet for his thoughts, or moulds the clay to his mood. He is brought, as it were, face to face with himself, and when we study the creative products of the child we gain insight into his growth.

In the following examples we see how the experiences of children handling materials have contributed to their growth as persons.

Wendy was an academically gifted child. On entering school she was a fluent reader, she could write a letter or compose a poem, she understood numbers and could manipulate them mentally with amazing rapidity. She had come to believe that she was more intelligent than any other child of her age and expected to succeed in everything she did. Other children found her difficult to play with. Her vivid imagination devised rules they couldn't follow. She was often left out of group play, and when this happened she retreated to books where she knew she was safe.

It was some months before Wendy's teacher could interest her in clay, which Wendy condemned as 'messy stuff and very puddlesome'. Unexpectedly one day the lump of clay claimed her and she pursued her new-found interest with the intensity she brought to most of her experiences. She found the material difficult to handle and her attempts to shape a ballet-dancer crumbled as the clay dried. Frustrated, she flung the lump of clay into the bin. 'Nasty, messy clay,' she murmured, and after washing her hands she retired to the book corner.

Later in the week, Wendy went back to the clay. With more pleasure and considerable humility she tried again. This time she fashioned a square tile. She then raised the centre of the tile and shaped her dancer in relief. Again she was dissatisfied and destroyed what she had made. Several times within the next fortnight Wendy tried again with the clay. She approached it humbly, but with a growing sense of pleasure. The embossed tile which she ultimately produced gave her a greater sense of achievement than any experience she had had up to then in school. In clay she had met an unusual challenge, and her arrogance was modified. She was even prepared to recognise the skill of other children in using the same material. Gradually Wendy turned more and more to the exploration of materials which challenged her. Her relationship with her fellow-workers was very much improved, and she really found fun in sharing the experience with others.

Linda, on the other hand, was academically weak. She was nearly eight before she could read and she made no attempt to write spontaneously. She loved sewing and was very clever with her fingers. She liked, most of all, to make wardrobes for her doll.

One day Linda said she would make a fashion book. On the first page of her book she pasted scraps of materials suitable for various garments and quoted the prices of them. She then described a wardrobe for her doll, Sally, making a tiny paper pattern for each item and calculating the cost of it. With scraps of material she made a picture of each finished piece of clothing. Her completed book she called 'I Sew for my Dolly'. Although the contents depended considerably on pictures, it was a most attractively illustrated story of her doll's wardrobe. A considerable amount of arithmetic had gone into it as well. Using a mode of communication which came easily to her and materials with which she felt at home, Linda had written her first book and it was given an honoured place amongst others on the library shelf.

5

The education of taste

Mrs D. was worried. 'How is it,' she said, 'that my children seem to have such crude ideas about the things they choose? I'm quite ashamed of their rooms and hope no one will think that they're brought up in a home lacking in good taste.'

What is good taste? Are children born with good or bad taste? Has taste anything to do with education? As Jeffreys says in *Personal Values in the Modern World*, 'The trouble with many people whose taste is bad is that they have never really encountered the best things.'

Taste is not easy to define. It is highly individual, varying from group to group and from one country to another. It would seem to be associated with fashion, and the tastefully-arranged drawing-room of a Victorian household would be quite unacceptable today.

Taste is associated with discrimination, with the ability to decide between the artistic and refined, and the inartistic and garish. Those things which are of good taste satisfy and give pleasure to our senses; but what pleases the eyes, ears and fingers of one person may offend the senses of another. Who is to decide? Each person recognises as beautiful those things which please him and to which he responds in positive emotional ways.

Widely as people differ in their choice of what pleases them, there are some objects which appeal to practically everyone. Good form is always satisfying and usually recognisable, and as nature is an expert in good form natural form is universally acceptable.

Shape depends on the relationship between material and function. In nature every shape is that which is the most effective under the circumstances. The smooth contours of a snail's shell are the result of the skill of creating, from fine material, a protective home for a spineless body. The cells of a honeycomb are brilliant examples of compactness and strength. The shape of a tree, with its spiralling arrangement of leaves, is so designed that each leaf has access to sun and rain. Nature always has a purpose and usually manages to combine beauty, strength and function.

Many of man's most pleasing designs echo natural form. The traditional jug is a good example, echoing the highly satisfying shape of the pear.

Taste could be said to be acquired, something the child learns, and the type of taste he acquires depends on the environment in which he has learned to discriminate. Like other aspects of learning, taste in the young child is immature and profoundly affected by the stage of development of the sense organs. A young child might combine colours which an adult would consider highly displeasing, because his eyes are as yet uneducated and unable to respond with the discrimination of adults.

The environment will decide what the child becomes accustomed to, and the choices he has learned to live with during his early experiences will influence his choices in later life. Many of our children come from homes where beauty is not considered important, and where each object must serve a 'useful' function. Something purchased 'just for the sake of having it' would be considered a waste of money. Such homes are not necessarily in the poorer and deprived areas. There are many middle-class homes whose aridity is not due to lack of money. In fact, works of art are sometimes purchased merely on the grounds that people of standing should display them in their homes. It is in the attitude of some people to the very things they possess that aridity lies. On the other hand, genuine appreciation of the worthwhile and beautiful can be found in homes of every social group. Indeed, the treasured possessions found in some of our poorest homes are enhanced by the drabness of their surroundings. What influences the child most powerfully is the way the adults he depends on behave towards their surroundings. If mother's reaction to orchestral music transmitted by radio or television is to switch it off or even to leave it on while she continues to talk at the top of her voice, how can the child learn to listen, let alone to grow sensitive to the artistic use of sound? The child's ears have become accustomed to harsh sounds in conflict with occasional musical sounds. The only way to reduce the conflict is to switch off the musical sound which he regards as an interruption.

One mother, a pleasant and sensitive parent, visited the classroom where the teacher was arranging a display of 'Things made of Glass'. The teacher held up a beautifully-curved bowl in blue glass which she was about to place on the display, and smiled at the mother. 'Isn't it lovely?' she said. 'Do you like it?'

The mother smiled in response, but her eyes were puzzled. 'Yes,' she agreed, 'it's very pretty. But what's it for?' The teacher's explanation meant very little, and while the mother didn't dislike such objects she clearly thought that they were a waste of time in the classroom.

Another parent was more aggressive. 'In my day,' he said, 'we might have a stuffed owl to look at for nature, but we learned something from it.'

No doubt the children learned something practical about glass and glass-blowing from the teacher who set out her display of glass, and the message of the display lay partly in its indication of the way man handles the material and of the uses he makes of glass. But the intrinsic value of her display went far deeper into the heart of things. The sheer wonder of the interplay of light and material, the form of the objects displayed and their colouring stirred those who could appreciate, reminding them that there is more to life than merely living.

On entering school children have already learned to respond in habitual ways to their surroundings. Fortunately they are still learning and their senses are in an undeveloped state, and they can still become sensitive in a way that will remain a part of their personalities. They can learn how to let their senses bring them joy for the rest of their lives. They can discover that other dimension to life which helps man to remain aware of his spiritual nature.

Each of us has the same range of senses. Since whatever affects the senses is stored in the mind, the more we satisfy the senses, the more satisfied the mind becomes. Those conditions in our surroundings which give pleasure to more than one of our senses at a time bring us the greatest joy. Good form, more than any other aspect of aesthetics, is likely to satisfy these conditions, and offering children these conditions is an essential part of their learning opportunity. The environment we live in becomes our life, and an essential responsibility of the teacher is to ensure that the aesthetic aspect of the child's surroundings is prized and respected.

The problem of teaching taste lies in its individual nature. We do not want to indoctrinate. The child must be free to become aware in his unique way. How then do we decide what to put before children? By what criteria do we select materials and objects which help him to become more sensitive?

The only safe guide a teacher has is her own pleasure. She selects what pleases her, and her genuine enjoyment of what she appreciates speaks to the children. She lets them see how she responds, and the sincerity of her feelings provides the right conditions for the children's growth as individuals.

The way in which material is presented is as important as the material itself. Just putting good material there is not enough; it isn't fair to children, whose senses may be largely unawakened, to expose them without preparation to objects of value. We cannot expect them to become sensitive overnight and the careful introduction of material will determine the effect it has on the children. The teacher may need to build up protective attitudes to what she displays before she can leave the children free to experience it.

One teacher was highly appreciative of design in pottery, and she had collected for use in her own home jugs, cups, dishes and so on which pleased her by their form. She decided to share these with her children and one day she brought to school her favourite milk jug. The traditional pear shape, so appropriate for containers of this kind, was executed to perfection in pale blue and grey pottery, and the lovely sheen on the glazing lifted the humble object into a special class.

Towards the end of the afternoon, when the children gathered round for their quiet time before leaving for home, the teacher produced her jug. 'This is my favourite cream jug,' she told them. 'When I go home for my tea, I like to have it on the table with the cups and plates which go with it.' The children murmured their agreement; they liked their teacher and were ready to approve of anything which she approved of. The teacher carried them a stage further.

'Why do you think I like it so much?' she asked. The children suggested, 'Because it pours the milk out!' Then one child offered her comment. 'It just looks nice,' she said. 'Can I hold it?' She was given the jug, and her face sparkled as her small hands wrapped round its pleasing form. Other children wanted to handle the jug, and eventually the teacher promised, 'Tomorrow I will bring some other things to go with it. I will leave them on this table and you can enjoy them with your eyes and with your hands.' There was no need for her to add, 'Please take care of them for me.' The children understood

43

what these objects meant to their teacher. They respected them because they were hers and because they enjoyed them too.

On another occasion a teacher set out a display of stainless steel and crystal against a pure white background. The effect was startlingly lovely and the children viewed it with awe. The teacher joined them, not to probe them into discussion, but to share with them the sheer pleasure of seeing the gleam and sparkle of polished steel, rock crystal and cut-glass. To enjoy was enough; the questions would come later.

Where objects of aesthetic value are to be left about the school more definite steps must be taken to protect them. The school service is an appropriate time in which to introduce such material and establish the right attitude towards it, before leaving it available for the children to enjoy. Pottery can be introduced as the product of loving hands, natural objects as things we are given to make life beautiful. The work of artists and masters of all kinds of materials can be appreciated as examples of what man's gifts can achieve. All aspects of natural beauty, all aspects of man's skill in handling materials can be included. There is aesthetic value in culinary equipment, in architecture, in decorative fabrics, as well as in fine paintings. There is beauty in rough unhewn rocks and crumbling soil, as well as in waterfalls and beech leaves.

A sense of purpose enhances a display of materials, and any display should contain a message which communicates itself readily to the observer, such as man's enjoyment and use of natural form; man's use of glass or clay; the pleasure of mathematical precision; shape in nature; the relationship between light and water.

Simplicity is essential. A cluttered environment kills beauty. Hoards of lovely things can over-stimulate and sicken the observer. No message can come through if a thousand other messages swamp it. A single well-arranged display will say more to the child than a museum of precious objects. Selection is an essential part of discrimination, and the beauty and pleasure of uncluttered simplicity are in themselves a relief to the soul.

In this aspect of the child's education the school has a responsible role. In school, the child can find opportunities to encounter the curious and the beautiful, sometimes for the first time. He may not at this stage fully understand, but he can feel in the deepest parts of him that pleasurable freedom of the spirit which constitutes the very essence of his living.

6

Developing sensitivity to
the worthwhile

Real feeling can only grow spontaneously. We cannot super-
vise children into feeling; they need to be alone with the
wonders of life in order to discover and know them.

Some schools recognise this need by providing a room, or a
corner apart, as a 'quiet room'. This is an environment rich in
aesthetic opportunity. The work of the masters, displays of
good form or colour or materials, objects to satisfy the senses
can be set apart in a place where children can come alone and
unsupervised, to make their own relationship with what they
find.

The aesthetic environment may not in itself hold a young
child's attention for any length of time, and provision is made
in the 'quiet room' for children to occupy themselves with
quiet pursuits within the cultural setting. Books, sewing,
puzzles, and perhaps music-making interest the children, who
learn to appreciate this peaceful retreat from the more
vigorous activity in the rest of the school.

The reactions of children to aesthetic experiences are
immature, and it takes time for feeling and sensitivity to
develop. Moreover we can never be sure what children learn
from these experiences. A picture illustrating a Henry Moore
sculpture, 'The Family', occupied a corner of one 'quiet room'.
Two little girls who visited it daily stood seemingly entranced

by the spectacle of this weird green sculpture, with its sinister cracked surface. Eventually their teacher enquired hopefully, 'You've come to look at this picture every day this week. Do you like it?' The little girls glanced at one another and squirmed. 'No,' they replied in unison.

'Then why do you stand looking at it?' their teacher asked in some surprise.

'Because it scares us,' they replied.

Their daily dose of fear was a part of their emotional development. Fear and excitement are closely linked, but so are fear and awe, and they in turn are linked with wonder and worship. The fear and fascination experienced by the little girls could well provide the foundation for respectful appreciation later on.

Mere exposure to the worthwhile does not necessarily help a child to become sensitive. Most children need positive and direct assistance from their teachers in building up sound attitudes towards things of value.

The attitude of the teacher matters more than anything else. The respect she pays to works of art and to the worthwhile in its many diverse forms will influence the children most profoundly.

A prerequisite of sensitivity is imagination, and imagination is a universal factor in creative work of any kind. It has been called by Wordsworth 'the heightened state of sensibility'. Imagination enables us to create a fresh idea by rearranging the images we already possess. We could describe it as the creative use of imagery, and the quality of imagination depends on the richness of the images it handles. Images are memories of perception; each experience registered through the senses is stored in their shape.

We can help children to see, hear and feel in such a way that the quality of their images is improved. Accuracy of observation is part of education. In other words, images can be taught. Vivid and accurate images provide the imagination with good material and the quality of a child's imaginative activity depends on the vitality and reality of his experiences.

Imagination and intellect are closely related. Without imagination thought is arid and understanding is superficial. When we are faced with a problem imagination helps us to recall previous experience, to see its relevance to the immediate situation and to anticipate the effects of action. Imagination, indeed, surpasses reasoning.

One aspect of the discovery approach to learning is the demands it makes on the child's imagination. Left to face his materials alone, the child finds his senses challenged. His discoveries are personal and vivid, unexpected and exciting; he is called upon to work on his environment and to create his secret world according to the way he sees it. He is in control and what he finds is his. His world extends as far as his imagination will take him.

> 'Know you what it is to be a child?...
> It is to believe in love
>   to believe in loveliness
>   to believe in belief...
>   it is to turn pumpkins into coaches
>   and mice into horses
>   lowness into loftiness
>   and nothing into everything.'
>
>   P. B. Shelley.

The child's imagination needs to grow as other aspects of him grow, and an experience of solitude from time to time is essential. Important as stimulation by others is to him, he needs time apart if the exquisite qualities of imagination are to unfold.

This doesn't mean that we must always stand by, afraid of interfering. Imagination is no delicate or metaphysical quality. It is vigorous and strong, and it needs feeding adequately and at regular intervals. There is much a teacher can do in the way of feeding in the material of the child's imagination, by giving him experience of a variety of lovely things and by showing him the imaginative work of other people.

In selecting such material the teacher is again guided by what moves her to feeling. Authoritative critics can help us to be perceptive about the creative work of other people, but they cannot make us feel, nor can they tell us how we ought to feel. What we enjoy and appreciate is entirely our own business, and children readily respond to genuine appreciation on our part. If we try to introduce them to poetry or pictures or fine sculpture which we ourselves do not enjoy, they readily recognize the synthetic quality of our recommendation.

As adults, we may be able to recall the moment when poetic delight was revealed to us. Often we owe the opening of magic casements to some adult we admired because of his burning enthusiasm for words. The poet and the child have much in common, for the child is essentially a sensitive person and the poet writes from the heart of his own feelings, etching them in a vivid explosion of sound and imagery. The young child who has just discovered his mother tongue and delights in the game of it, the nine-year-old in complete mastery of this tongue and revelling in his use of words, are both fully alive to the excitement of the poet. What does a poem like this do for such a child?

> The upper skies are palest blue,
>> Mottled with pearl and fretted snow:
> With tattered fleece of inky hue
>> Close overhead the storm-clouds go.
> Their shadows fly along the hill
>> And o'er the crest mount one by one,
> The whitened planking of the mill
>> Is now in shade and now in sun.'
>>>> *The Upper Skies.* Robert Bridges.

– or this?

> Dirty British coaster with salt-caked smoke stack
> Butting through the Channel in the mad March days,
> With a cargo of Tyne coal,
> Road-rails, pig-lead,
> Firewood, iron-ware, and cheap tin trays.

Cargoes. John Masefield.

We can offer the best to children with confidence. Meaning is conveyed as much by the emotional quality of the words and images as by the actual words used. Imagination offers a means of comprehending which intellectual reasoning alone can never supply. We share what we love with the child and he interprets it at his own level of maturity.

Stories spark imagination by enlarging experience; they mirror life and extend the child's understanding of it. Fairy tales are by no means the most suitable form of story for this purpose. Myths and legends open up the magic of the ages, stories of travel and adventure wing the child away beyond the bounds of the world he knows, stories of today and yesterday are as exciting as the science fiction of tomorrow. The teacher must read many stories, and those which stay with her, the ones she can read again and again with ever-increasing enjoyment, are the ones she can safely share with children.

Often the artist in action appeals more directly to children than do the works of art he produces. The four-year-old child who sits at the feet of her father as he practises his violin will be moved to the heart when, as an adult, she hears the violin played. Many teachers have artistic gifts, they write poetry or stories, they play musical instruments, they paint or model. Little can compare with watching the imagination of another person at work. The teacher who shares her own gifts with children may fire the imagination of a child who might otherwise remain untouched.

In some schools we find that pieces of sculpture are part of the construction of the building. Imagination on the part of those responsible for designing and executing the building the child works in provides inspiration to generations of children. The very recognition of such works as an important part of their learning environment is eloquent.

From time to time even the younger children can be taken by an enthusiastic teacher to see a play produced by professionals in a 'real' theatre. The sense of occasion and the atmosphere of theatre life in themselves stimulate imaginative activity on the part of the child. The play they see may be forgotten, but the image and magic of the theatre will remain.

John Neville, working in the Nottingham Playhouse, believed that children learn to appreciate the theatre by being involved in production themselves. He formed a small team of actors who visited schools and performed extracts from classics like *Julius Caesar*. The children helped by taking small parts and appearing in crowd scenes. Thus children rehearsed with the experts and later staged the play for the school. They were enabled to discover from the inside what acting was about.

John Neville also organised regular matinées for children in the Playhouse. As the children grew older they could join the theatre club, 'Youth Workshop', which met on Saturday mornings to discuss theatre with the experts and to learn the art of acting. They heard professional actors talking about their work and learned to appreciate the theatre through their own creative efforts.

Visits to museums, art galleries and monuments can enrich the inner life of the child in many ways. Often, however, the younger child will gain as much and sometimes more from finding in the familiar school environment a few examples selected from such collections. An axe-head borrowed by the teacher from the local museum and handled, or even used, by the child in his own classroom can stir his mind more actively than a complete collection of prehistoric tools viewed in the museum itself.

There are endless opportunities for the teacher to create a fertile environment which will enable the child's imagination to unfold and flourish. He may then develop the capacity to perceive and comprehend the real and full value of what he encounters; he will have the opportunity to discover and express a world which exists in his own mind.

7

Appreciating the work of the masters

At the age of seven Sarah was fascinated by a print of a Botticelli painting representing the Madonna. She spent many patient hours trying to reproduce her impressions of this picture. If someone had asked her to say why she liked the picture, she would have found it difficult to explain in words. This picture was one of a set called 'The World's Hundred Best Pictures', and she had found the set rolled in a cardboard cylinder in her grandmother's spare room. Some of the pictures she thought quite useless and wondered why the painter had ever bothered to make them. A few she loved, and of these the Madonna became her favourite. She was many years older before she knew that its creator was a famous artist, and this information confirmed the extraordinary quality she had recognized from the first moment she saw it.

The work of the artist is a part of the environment inherited by the child. Sometimes a child like Sarah can discover the artist's touch unaided, provided it is available. Other children may need the help of an adult and it is difficult to decide at what age to focus the attention of the child more definitely on work we consider to be artistic. The child may be surrounded from birth by the best in creative work, and he will sense the appreciation of adults through the way they respect these treasures. But he may very well need more positive guidance towards such material before he can enter into the mind of the artist and lose himself there.

A simple way of introducing nursery-age children to pictures of value is to mount the postcard prints sold in art shops on stout tinted card. These can be kept in a box or spread over a table. Children can handle them, selecting those they enjoy, talk to one another about them, or simply look at them as they would the illustrations in a book. Inexpensive art books of the works of such artists as Manet, Gauguin or Van Gogh can be included in the library corner or associated with displays in the school. Children in the Infant School, working with an enthusiastic teacher, may have learned to recognise and appreciate the work of a number of artists. They may enjoy the exciting colours used by Gauguin, Manet's use of blue, or the vivid quality of Van Gogh's painting; and they will learn to recognise the work of each artist wherever they may find it.

The school pianist is often well acquainted with the life and work of musicians. In some schools small groups of children gather round the school pianist while she tells them, with illustrative examples, about the life of Mozart.

Andy was a difficult boy with a disturbing home background, but music appealed to him and his aggressive behaviour disappeared when he listened to it. He enjoyed the responsibility of selecting music for the school service; he treated the record-player with gentle respect and could be trusted to operate it with great skill. With the school pianist he was completely amenable and attended her talks regularly.

The work of great musicians plays an important part in the school service, sometimes to establish a mood of worship as the children assemble, sometimes to terminate the service. The appreciation of man's most skilful use of sound can become the focal part of a service. Works such as Mozart's 'Eine Kleine Nachtmusik' provide in themselves a spiritual experience. Associating them with time set aside for worship helps the child to experience the respect due to them.

Displays of the best in creative work of all kinds, in wood, metal, stone, and fabric, have already been considered. Collections of 'Poems We Love' contain extracts, sometimes little more than phrases, from the works of the great poets. In one classroom a book of 'Words We Remember' contained words such as 'filigree', 'mollusc', 'caterwauling', 'effigies' and 'zodiac', all words the children had collected from poetry read to them by the teacher.

The most powerful form of understanding comes through personal involvement. Creative experiences enable us to appreciate the creativity of the artist. Only those who have tried to express an inner vision or feeling in paint, who have struggled with clay to mould it into an expression of themselves, or who have sweated with words to formulate their thoughts, can really know what happens between the master and his materials.

Children at their own level can explore materials creatively. The spontaneous, unsophisticated creativity of children often comes nearer the work of the artist than the more disciplined, self-conscious efforts of adults. The child, through his own efforts, grows into his culture, and the crudity of his attainments brings him into sympathy with the masters who have shared the same experiences.

The child of four or five will make himself one-note tunes. Sometimes he sings his tune, 'I am John. I am John. I can hop'. Sometimes he plays his tunes on a drum, a tambourine, or a chime bar. Often such tunes are accompanied by movement and can provide starting points for movement themes and group dances. With the help of a flannelgraph staff and notes, children can record their tunes and in this way repeat the experience or share it with others. The following extract from a book of 'Tunes We Have Made' indicates how a five-year-old made and recorded her own composition:

'Lin   da   Wing
I can play my name.'

The sea is a universal source of excitement and inspiration. The following poems, written by children of different ages, reflect development in the quality of their poetic use of words.

'The sea is rushing up the rocks and down the rocks and washing all the sand and the sun is sparkling on the sea.'

(By a child aged six.)

'John's Poem about the Sea

The sea's face is bluey green,
When it is grey, then it wants me so much as though
                    I was its father.
The waves toss for me and I would toss for them
                    and it calls for me.
I have something in me for the sea
It does toss and toss for me so much
That it would drown itself for me.'

(By a child aged nine.)

' The Sea Serpent

Luminous sea serpent
Deep in the murk
Of phosphorescent waters
Body rippling up and down
With a smooth and supple grace
No light to lighten his territories
Save ghostly luminosity.

On the surface
The moon embraces the earth
With a grip of silver light:
But down in the sea serpent's home
All is black
Save for his luminosity.'

(By a child aged eleven.)

Many examples of the way in which children create, using words, notes, numbers and other materials, are quoted throughout these books on young children learning. The completely uninhibited exploration of materials often takes place beyond the more controlled situation of the classroom. A children's art club is run by students in some colleges, perhaps on Saturday mornings and usually on college premises. Great freedom of expression is often observed here, and materials are frequently used in very unorthodox ways.

For instance, many kinds of marking media such as onion or beetroot water, a solution of permanganate of potash, the petals of marigold flowers crushed to a paste, are used as often as paint, chalk, crayon or charcoal. The spokes of a bicycle wheel were used by two children to create a three-dimensional picture. Children can spread sheets of brown paper or sacking over the floor and experiment with enamel paint, poster colour or coloured inks, applying these media in many ways, such as flipping or trailing a laden brush or blowing ink from a bottle.

Whatever the media, whether in the form of words, colour or sound, the combination of the child's natural need to explore and the impressions he receives of the use made of these media by the masters, fosters understanding and awareness of genuine artistry. The master shows the child what is possible, and the child discovers for himself the difficult experience which gave expression to those possibilities.

8

The growth of the spirit

On his first day in school Fred was given a giant red pencil-crayon and a piece of paper. He scribbled until his paper was a solid mass of red wax. He then went into the book corner and extended the same treatment to one of the new and beautifully illustrated picture books. He had no means of discriminating between the two situations.

Many teachers are faced with problems of this kind. Children like Fred have had no chance to develop respect and the ability to discriminate because they come from homes where adults are indifferent to these values. School is their first experience of a way of life in which good attitudes can develop. Fortunately the teacher of young children can have a profound and beneficial influence on minds in the making. On entering school the child is still very dependent on adults and often finds in his teacher unexpected outlets for his personal development. His teacher represents for him the first adult of importance beyond the family group. She is his introduction to society outside the home, and through her he has access to the cultural inheritance of the society in which his family lives. She is responsible for transmitting to him the artistic and cultural accomplishments of his race. It is she who can open up those aspects of his life which will encourage his spirit to grow.

It is not only the child from the culturally poor background who benefits from his relationship with the teacher. Children from good backgrounds may remain undeveloped in many ways within the family group. Because the teacher is a different person and in an influential position, she can liberate aspects of the child's personality which have so far remained dormant. Her personality is a challenge to his developing person. For the first time in his life the young child is considerably free of dependence on his home and family. He has a chance to know himself as an individual, against the background of his family, as well as being part of it.

In his new-found freedom the child is highly sensitive to the attitudes and enthusiasms of the significant people he meets outside his home. Through them he gains a fresh view of himself. His teacher sees him not as a mother would but as a person in authority who is anxious to discover what he has to offer to society. The child responds with increasing awareness of his own person. There are fresh things he can be, and an added sense of being grows in him. The secret parts of his personality find expression, and he is no longer simply part of a family. He is unique, a person in his own right, with an independent life to lead and an inner vision of life which no one has the power to violate.

This liberation of the spirit is the first responsibility of the teacher and of the environment she provides. The child's growing sense of self-awareness is closely connected with the kind of person the teacher is and the type of experience she offers him. The beautiful in life and the work of the masters are part of the learning situation established in school. The materials the teacher provides for the child are equally important, for it is in the materials he uses that the child finds out about himself and discovers dormant aspects of his personality.

Outside of the school the family remains the most powerful influence over the child, but there are many other pressures bringing their influence to bear upon him, and perhaps the most important of these are the various forms of mass media the child encounters in the present-day world. Here again he needs help in learning how to discriminate between the worthwhile and the trivial or detrimental, and he doesn't always get the help he needs from his home.

Mark, aged four, loved painting. Each day he painted bold pictures in vivid colours, and central to all of these pictures was a huge eye. When asked about his pictures, Mark pointed to the eye and said, 'That's telly.' Eventually his teacher discovered that Mark's bed had been sold and he slept on the settee in the living-room. Each night he dropped off to sleep watching the television set, which dominated the cramped living-room and which was left on until the stations closed down.

Technicians have given us many wonderful channels of communication. Although twenty-nine per cent of all homes in this country have only five, or even fewer, books, according to the Plowden Report, few are without radio and television. In many of these homes only the television set speaks in sentences, and although these sentences are scarcely heeded, they remain a perpetual influence. When vision reinforces the experience of sound, the influence is at its maximum, and the possibility of the child becoming accustomed to other-direction at the expense of self-direction is increased.

No form of mass medium is, in itself, a detrimental influence. The terrifying trend towards all people being fed with the same facts at the same time can be opposed by the developing powers of discrimination. By establishing a sense of values and helpful attitudes in the nation's future citizens, education can ensure that mass forms of communication are an asset and become part of the education of the individual.

One group of six to seven-year-old children share ten minutes 'television time' with their teacher every day. Programmes that the teacher and children have seen are discussed, and forthcoming programmes considered. Thus the attention of the children is directed towards programmes they find interesting and helpful. If a child goes home knowing which programme he wants to see, the family as a rule switches it on for him. Some highly profitable interests have as a result been developed by this group of children.

At one point their imagination was caught by an air display, in which aeroplanes of all vintages performed. Five boys developed an interest in flight because they were fascinated by the different shapes of the aeroplanes, and they then turned their attention to 'other things that flew through the air'. Birds and missiles, meteors and raindrops, parachutes and helicopters were taken up in turn. With some help from their teacher they selected television programmes which would further these interests, and much of their information was acquired by viewing. A science programme which offered suggestions for experimentation helped them to understand some of the basic principles of flight.

The same teacher encourages these children to watch and criticise the commercials. Chocolate beans and sugar puffs, crisps and iced-lollies are measured carefully against the claims made by manufacturers on television. Critical observers of the future are less likely to fall prey to persuasive salesmen, and these are young citizens who are learning to debunk unscrupulous advertisers.

As children become fluent readers, they should be given help with the material they meet in newspapers and magazines. They need to know how news is reported, edited and printed, so that they can assess the value of what they read. When they understand the powerful role played by the press, they will know how to interpret what is printed. It is as important to learn what to read and how to read it, as it is to learn to read.

Other forms of mass media such as the cinema are less likely to be an influence because they are less frequently encountered. The most widespread form of mass communication is the book, and the school has a clear responsibility for what the child reads both outside and inside the school. Out-of-school reading may, indeed, account for a considerable amount of the child's total reading. Teachers who encourage children to bring their own books, magazines and papers to school can see what is read and offer helpful suggestions and, sometimes, criticism. Parents are usually grateful for the advice of teachers when buying books for their children. A display of suitable books and a discussion one evening towards Christmas time will help parents to spend their money wisely. Too often a book is bought for its jacket rather than for its contents.

Children who develop a wealth of interests and have acquired the habit of initiating their own activities have great resources available to them during leisure hours. Education for leisure is as important as education for vocation or for home-making. In adult life it is in his leisure hours that man can find time to renew, each day, his acquaintance with his own spirit, but sources of spiritual refreshment are available only to those who have learned how to use them. The negative experiences we inevitably meet each day can have no effect on the person who possesses his spiritual self. The person who has developed those personal values by which he is able to recognise and measure the quality of any situation or thing is protected against the adverse influence of the synthetic, the trivial and the destructive. He knows what is real. He is also able to recognise in another person that same spirit and so experiences that communion between people in which each becomes more deeply aware of life's inner dimensions.

Discrimination and appreciation go hand in hand, and it is often left to the school to develop these powers in children. For many children school can open up vistas they may have no chance of glimpsing otherwise.

9

The foundation of belief

In the modern Primary School, where adults and children work closely together in a creative environment, religious education is not a period on the timetable but a way of living and part of the life teachers and children share. The sheer delight of the child in what he discovers fills him with wonder and brings him to the brink of worship. Service is an opportunity for sharing these experiences with one another in the presence of God.

The whole life of the Primary School is created by the personal relationships which develop in it, and the quality of personal communion which exists in the school stems from that activity we call service. A description of some of the ways in which service is interpreted will illustrate this situation.

In many schools one service each week is set aside for sharing the 'things we have made'. In one school this service is also an occasion in which parents can participate. About a dozen parents attend, often of course the parents of children whose work is displayed as the focal point of appreciation. Over the year a large proportion of parents find themselves involved in this way.

'Care of others' was the theme for a whole week in the services held in one Infant School. The children made and brought pictures, they composed their own prayers and selected suitable poems and extracts from the psalms, they suggested stories for the head teacher to read. On one occasion the caretaker, who was also a pianist, offered to play the familiar tunes for the hymns the children had chosen. The school secretary and some of the women who cooked and served dinner or who cared for the children during lunchtime also joined the service. In fact the whole of the school community shared in the expression of this theme. Some of the prayers indicated a real, if immature, concern for others:

'Dear God please help me to be kind to people who are sick and fall down and hert themselves. When they fall down and hert themselves and start to cry I help them to there mother.'

'Please God help me to grow up in to a nice mother and do nice things for my children.'

In the life of the school, service of this kind is a means of integrating relationships. It is an activity shared by people whose ages range from four to sixty. It is a time for giving and taking among adults and children alike.

The 1944 Act requires each school to begin the day with an act of corporate worship. There are many ways of interpreting this regulation, and it may be found that other times in the day are often more appropriate, or that all children in the school may take part in service at the same time but not necessarily in the same place. Small intimate groups in different parts of the building may provide the feeling of 'where two or three are gathered together' in a way which is impossible when the whole school is involved. In one school the headmistress held a voluntary service on one day in the week. A cow bell warned the school of the time of Service, and children came in small family groups from different parts of the school. The atmosphere of a voluntary service has a quality not found in the routine service.

The atmosphere of service can be established before the children enter the hall. One headmistress set out an embroidered

Indian rug and a polished wooden table. The children selected objects they treasured from displays in the school and arranged them on the table or rug. In this way they prepared a focal point for service time. Good music introduced and terminated the event.

Sources of inspiration take a number of forms. Sometimes a teacher may bring a curious or beautiful object, a length of lovely material, a book or a record, around which the service might centre. The sharing of experience and of the successful accomplishments of adults and children can also inspire wonder and reverence.

In one Infant School the headmistress invited children from all parts of the school to bring things they had made for a display in the hall. As part of service, she asked some of the children to tell the whole school about their exhibits.

Vivienne, an agile six-year-old, accompanied Kevin and Jane to the hall where Kevin's ingenious robot and Jane's embroidered Wendy House table-cloth were carefully displayed. The headmistress asked Vivienne, 'Did you bring anything?' Vivienne shook her head defensively. 'No,' she said. 'I wanted to make a doll's pram but the wheels fell off. I never make good things with my hands.'

There was a short silence. Then the headmistress remembered Vivienne's supple body in movement lessons. 'Why, you do,' she told her. 'I've watched you in movement. Your hands make beautiful pictures all by themselves'.

Vivienne's hands responded, and pleasure lit her face. 'Do you really think so?' she asked. She showed no trace of regret or resentment when Kevin and Jane showed their work to the school.

The next morning in the service, the headmistress developed the idea of individual differences and of how parents and teachers, like God, are glad that each child is different because each one is beautiful in some special way. Then she told them about Vivienne's pram, and asked Vivienne to show the other children how, even when her body was still, her hands danced in beautiful patterns. Those hands might be unable to make the wheels stay on the pram, but they excelled in making lovely shapes.

After the service some of the children stayed behind to talk to the headmistress. Amongst them was Judy, who explained that she wasn't good at sewing, but that she made the very best jam tarts. She asked if she could bring some of these for the display. It is in ways like these that children are helped to accept and respect themselves; they are then in a position to understand and be concerned about others.

Spiritual ideas are the most abstract and difficult of all concepts to formulate. Children acquire from adults a vocabulary of words which represent spiritual concepts, but we must not assume that the meaning they attach to these terms is either complete or deep. Ronald Goldman, in his book *Religious Thinking from Childhood to Adolescence*, warns us against the 'danger for the child of acquiring a religious vocabulary which has no conceptual substance'. Using such a vocabulary, to which the child may attach superficial and even inaccurate meaning, will lead to shallow thinking, and the child's concepts will remain as shallow as his thoughts.

The spiritual development of the child is closely interwoven with his emotional life. Young children have a capacity for perfect feeling. Such moments of pure emotion are rarely echoed in adult life. It is through his feelings that the child understands, and what he believes in later life is founded on the way he feels about things.

If a child has confidence in a parent or teacher he is willing to share with them his most profound experiences. The understanding teacher will be more concerned to encourage children to talk about the things that matter to them than about telling them Bible stories which centre around adult concepts. The illness of a pet, the death of a grandmother, the lovely colours of the rainbow – these are experiences which stir a child deeply. If he can talk to his teacher about them and with her help come to terms with his feelings and learn how to express and communicate them, then he is able to reach through to the heart of the matter and begin to understand what is real in life.

Death is an experience from which adults tend to protect children. The child's attitude to it is often different from that of the adult. A child may feel deprived by the death of his grandmother who used to bake delicious rock buns. He is upset by being separated from someone who loved him, but he can accept death itself as a natural process. He doesn't see it as a morbid event which he should avoid because it is frightening.

Children vary enormously in their reactions to events of this kind. One child may genuinely grieve because his mother is no longer alive, whereas another may be more concerned by the changes which take place in the home or by the fact that 'Auntie doesn't make dinner as nice as Mum did'. We can never assume that children view life and death as adults do. Like other ideas their concepts of life are immature and closely linked with personal experience and feelings.

Encouraging children to talk is a beginning, but as teachers we need to go further. The young child may not be able to be fully articulate about his feelings unless he can express them through materials as well as through words.

Hannah was puzzled when her mother produced a new brother. At the age of six she found it difficult to understand that her mother was absorbed in the baby and spent a lot of time looking after him. She wasn't sure, either, where baby Peter had come from and asked her mother to explain. Her mother told her, in simple terms, how Peter was first thought of and how he had arrived.

In school Hannah asked her teacher to make her a book, 'with a lot of pages and a nice blue cover', because she was making a book about a baby boy. Her book consisted of a series of pictures, accompanied by a few words, describing the way in which Peter developed inside his mother and then emerged as a baby. This experience enabled Hannah to come to terms with the event which brought a rival for her mother's attention. Her teacher knew and understood, and Hannah felt reassured.

Although the young child's concepts of life are immature, he does think and understand. Sometimes he asks penetrating questions which indicate his sensitivity to the spiritual aspects of his life. His thought and understanding are not at the adult level, but in his own way he is beginning to work things out for himself.

There is a stage, for instance, when a child begins to distinguish clearly between reality and fiction, and he asks 'Is it true?' He becomes aware of himself as an independent person and wants to know 'Where did I come from?', and, at a later stage, 'Why am I here?' He hears the terms 'God', 'Heaven', 'Holy Spirit', 'good', 'evil', 'conscience', and he begins to feel that they bear some relation to his existence and wants to fit them into his scheme of things: 'Who is God? What is Heaven like? What do evil people look like?', and so on.

When we answer these questions we must match the mood of the child asking them. We must guard against reading into the minds of children the thoughts which occupy ours. When a child asks about death he isn't suffering from a morbid obsession, he is naturally curious. His interest in sexual experiences is also part of his discovery of life. His questions about good and evil, heaven and hell, are part of his need to fit these things into his map of the world; and by labelling them clearly he can keep them in their right place. He needs to be in control of the situation, and he can only achieve this by identifying the things he finds.

The moral and mental health of the child depends basically on how he feels about other people. When he comes into school he is required to make considerable adjustments in learning how to become one of a group, and to make sound relationships with individuals. There is much the teacher of young children can do to help each child to develop sound and responsible attitudes towards other people. Moral standards are established through respect between persons, but the recognition of the rights of others is a difficult social lesson.

The child who respects himself is in a position to respect others. When he knows himself and likes what he knows he is free to give himself in friendship. The teacher who can help a child to feel acceptable and a worthwhile member of the group helps him to see himself as a desirable person. Some of our children are more favourably endowed than others, who may have fewer obvious gifts, a family background which has given them a poor self-image, or who may be temperamentally withdrawn and unable to present themselves to others.

Barry had four sisters, all older than himself. He was thin and undersized for his age and his eyes were weak. When he entered school his oldest sister was already a young woman of sixteen and the most dominant of Barry's five 'mothers'. All of the girls were academically competent, and because Barry was quiet and unobtrusive he was treated by the rest of the family as slow. His oldest sister explained to his teacher, 'He's a nice little kid, Miss, but you'll find he's not very bright.'

School gave Barry his first opportunity to escape from the overpowering influence of his family. His teacher encouraged him to talk and found time to listen to what he had to say, and for the first time in his life Barry felt able to hold the attention of a person he loved and respected. Self-confidence began to shine through his unobtrusive personality, and his face glowed with interest. Although he remained a quiet person he made many friends and developed powers of leadership.

One of the most encouraging things an adult can do for a child is to accept him. The teacher of young children in many ways represents to the child the attitude of society outside the home. The child sees in his teacher an adult in whose judgement he has complete faith. For a few children, who have been given an unfavourable view of themselves in their family circle, the teacher may be the first adult who makes them feel worthwhile.

An injury at birth had left Eric with a twisted neck. He moved in an ungainly manner and was regarded by his mother as a 'judgement on herself, because she'd tried to do away with him when she knew she was likely'. Eric's mishandled childhood had left him emotionally handicapped, and when he entered school his anti-social behaviour created perpetual problems. Fortunately he had a teacher who neither pitied nor despised him. She was interested in the cause of his trouble and her interest lent her the sympathy to treat him as a casualty rather than as a nuisance. His twisted personality began to respond. He appreciated her firm handling of him, and he loved her because she understood. Warm feeling for another person was an experience Eric had scarcely met in his home, and although it came too late to compensate completely for what amounted to maternal deprivation, there were at least times in school when Eric behaved like a normal child.

Along with acceptance goes understanding, and understanding helps a teacher to tolerate a very wide range of behaviour on the part of the child. She may even achieve the ability to remain undisturbed by unduly aggressive behaviour and other forms of emotional ill-health, and to provide the very stability the child needs when his own feelings make him 'beside himself'. The child's mental and emotional stability in school stems from the teacher's own serenity. For a child whose world is full of emotional conflict, simply experiencing the inner peace and harmony of someone who is important to him may help him to come to terms with his conflict and to acquire a measure of peace for himself. An undisturbed adult may, indeed, be a new experience for him.

The recognition and satisfaction of the child's needs as a person have full expression in the life of the schools of today. We know that children can learn to appreciate the creativity of the Maker only through adequate creative outlets of their own, and that to challenge a child's intellectual curiosity helps him to become aware of his intellectual gifts. The whole life of the school centres on helping the child to become fully aware of himself and so to appreciate the very stuff of life. It sometimes rests with the school to awaken the child to the spiritual nature of his life. More often than not, the job of the teacher in the school is complementary to the work of the home and of the child's own family; but all children should find in school the expression of some aspect of life which the home cannot cater for. One of the chief functions of schools and teachers is to open up possibilities for the child in every aspect of his physical and spiritual life.

Children live nearer to the creative centre than most adults. They have an aptitude for reaching through to the deep centre of things, where the conventional reasoning of adults creates a barrier. Children don't stop to ask whether this or that is possible, or why it is so: they believe and can accept many mysteries of life without question.

The young child is capable of a very wide range of feeling, and his impressions of the world are fresh enough to make each sensory response a very meaningful experience. In this pure form emotional experience comes very close to creativity. St. Matthew realised this and saw the ideal state as one of recapturing the child's simple oneness of spirit: 'Except ye become as little children'. As teachers, one of our greatest privileges is the opportunity we have to enter into a spiritual experience every time we share with the child his worship of the curious and beautiful world in which he finds himself.

10

Developing the child's creative gifts

Individuality is perhaps the most outstanding phenomenon of the human situation. Its significance underlies the whole of human behaviour. Each one of us prizes his unique qualities as a person, and recognition of what is unique in us gives us infinite pleasure and satisfaction. At birth individual differences make each child the only one of its kind, and as the child develops and adjusts to his individual environment, his unique nature is increasingly emphasised. Individuality is permanent. We remain who we are for the whole of a lifetime, and each change affecting personality reinforces our individual nature. Thus the more we change, the more like ourselves we become. So highly prized is this quality of being unique that if in a crowded room a person's name is mentioned, his immediate attention is assured. Small wonder, then, that in a liberal society the rights of a man to preserve his individuality are fundamental to the way of life described by the laws of that society.

Unique as we are at birth, it is through sharing life with other people that we develop as individuals. At first the baby is almost completely dependent, and so his individuality is fettered. His constant striving towards freedom starts at birth; his first cry is a demand for air so that he can breathe as a separate person. The umbilical cord is cut and from then on he

72

is urged to learn and by so doing to become independent. The need to establish himself as an individual who can survive in competition with others dominates his behaviour and ensures learning and development.

In the early stages of life the child learns to discriminate between himself and his mother. By feeling the shape of himself he discovers where his physical self begins, where he finishes and his mother begins. The idea of himself as a separate person becomes established, and he can then begin to acquire an impression of what he is like.

The child receives information about himself from other people. His mother tells him he is 'good' and she shows him she approves of him or that he can sometimes be 'naughty' and not the kind of child she wants him to be. Other people may tell him he is 'a beautiful boy', 'big for his age', 'clever', and so on. They show him by the way they treat him or respond to him what they think about him. Later, the mirror will describe what these terms mean and confirm the impression he has gained from these observations.

Fear is a basic drive in a child, and fear of being left alone by his mother drives him to be all she expects of him in order to secure her attention. Another thing a child learns at an early age is that his mother can identify him even when there are many other babies around. His relationship with her is on a one-to-one footing, and she treats him in a way which is special to him. The idea of himself as separate and different from everyone else is established early in life. As he grows older, he comes to realise that individuality is a responsibility, that he is entrusted with unique qualities and is responsible for ensuring the use of those qualities and for becoming himself in the fullest possible sense of the word.

As the child becomes familiar with materials he finds in what he does with them a further expression of his individuality. Everything he does, in fact, bears the stamp of his unique workmanship; the things he makes, the way he uses his tools, his handwriting, even the clothes he wears are signed by him in a unique manner. Later in life he learns that as a mature person he must take full responsibility for what he is and for all he does.

It is by sharing what he is with others that the child confirms himself to himself. As a person he needs to express his innermost thoughts and feelings. Only sincerity of expression brings him satisfaction, and using the ideas of other people results in shallow and unsatisfactory work. So important is the integrity of the individual that the law recognises his right to protect it; thus plagiarism or the stealing of ideas is penalised.

Peggy was the youngest of three. Her parents were understanding people and the home provided great freedom and many opportunities for the children to experiment. Peggy's older brothers had many hobbies. They kept mice and tropical fish, they visited the swimming baths, worked hard in their own piece of their father's garden and even built a miniature greenhouse in which they grew 'rare specimens'. Peggy was encouraged to share every activity and by the time she went to school she had an active mind well-stocked with information.

The school was pleasant but very formal. There was no sand or water, no dressing-up or pastry-making, no aquarium or pet corner; in fact, Peggy spent most of her time struggling to copy words from the blackboard and trying to interpret the patterns of words on paper. She recited her counting and her tables, and her teacher classified her as 'a nice enough child but very ordinary'. She had no idea at all about Peggy's experiences with mice and tropical fish, foreign stamps and cacti; nor did she know that Peggy could swim, mix and bake a fruit cake, and take cuttings from geraniums. Peggy tolerated school activities as something she was expected to do, but she found no opportunity there for offering herself or for sharing her interests and gifts with others.

The creatively-gifted teacher is not necessarily the person who enables children to be creative themselves. She may in her own creative enthusiasm tend to dominate a child, or at least to influence him in his work. A teacher who can detect a gift in a child and encourage him to develop it may watch a child create in a way she herself is quite incapable of doing. Her sympathy and insight will do more to help the child than her own creative talent.

Creating a helpful atmosphere depends on the personality of the teacher rather than on expensive equipment or inspirational situations. The teacher who can put the needs of the child before her own frees the child to express himself; but the teacher who views the work of the child in terms of the credit it will bring her, or who uses the work of the child to express her own ideas, seeks satisfaction for herself and the child is bound by her dominance. His efforts are dissipated by his desire to please his teacher, and her approval or disapproval dominates the result.

The atmosphere most conducive to creative work is one in which the child feels free to communicate with his materials in his own way, without undue concern about the outcome. He should not feel obliged to make anything or to satisfy anyone else but himself. He should feel assured of his teacher's undemanding interest in what he is doing, and of her sympathy with his problems. He should feel able to turn to her for advice, confirmation, or approval, but he should not feel pressed to adopt formal techniques or to conform to a pattern in shaping his materials.

A methodical approach to materials is helpful, and when a number of children work in close proximity a well-organised room is essential, but freedom to move about the room and beyond it helps to establish a feeling of freedom in expression. There should be respect for materials and a concern for their quality and condition; slivers of wood from orange boxes and hard lumps of clay will destroy creative interest. The teacher's own love of good materials in good condition and her own appreciation of an orderly environment will be far more effective in helping children to work in harmony than any number of rules.

The teacher who shares the child's joy in his own creative efforts is an inspiration to him. She must be equally receptive to his crude and immature efforts. Children who are free to follow their natural exploration of materials frequently startle the adult with the primitive reality of their results. The teacher who can accept the crude nature of the child's work is accepting a stage in the development of his creative expression, for often his work will reflect the crude reality of primitive man. The first uninhibited paintings of children shine amongst the more sophisticated efforts of older children or adults.

Creative expression develops in a child in much the same way as any other aspect of his ability develops. There is in man a primitive need to represent, to translate feelings and experiences into symbols which can be stored in the mind or recorded in visible form, and the child's early marks on paper are evidence of his need to symbolise. They are an expression of what he has discovered about his materials and the kind of relationship he is making with them. Symbols soon begin to appear amongst his marks, and he is then using his materials to fulfil his purpose. Scribbling has great significance, and with each kind of material the child goes through the scribble stage. An examination of the child's scribble reveals his interest in his surroundings and can be a guide to what he finds significant or disturbing. A child of five drew a picture of Daddy wearing shoes with enormous bows: at this stage in his development the tying of bows in shoelaces had great significance. A little girl of four drew a series of men with two heads. 'It's Uncle George,' she explained. 'Mum says he's double-faced.'

Certain symbols found amongst the child's scribble would seem to be archetypes. The figure of a man, for instance, is represented by a ball and sticks; childish pictures of houses have a universal pattern; the sun, trees, and many other objects are represented by symbols which most children adopt. Some of the same symbols often appear whether the child has seen them before or not.

A base-line appears at quite an early stage, and the sky is usually represented by a line at the top of the paper. Adults frequently tell children to fill in the sky and make it touch the ground, but from the child's point of view there is a space between the ground and the sky. The six-year-old may introduce more than one base line, and streets are frequently drawn with the houses flanking one side upside down. Pictures may take on a diagrammatic appearance and something intermediate in character between a picture and a map may represent 'What I saw on the way to school'.

When making pictures children aren't always concerned with sequence, and they will draw the past, present and future all happening at the same time. John getting his breakfast, going to school and coming home again may be represented in a single pictorial instant.

Children draw what they think and find no problem in showing both the outside of a house and its contents in the same picture. Often they dismay the teacher by washing black over the whole of a vivid picture because 'It's night,' or 'It's a foggy day'. They are more concerned with using the materials and in making them express what they feel or think than they are in producing a permanent result. They may be quite indifferent to the end-product.

Creative growth is part of total growth, and the child's creative work is often a guide to other aspects of his development. The child's picture of a man indicates his developing concept of man and is sometimes used as an index of intelligent observation. The way a child handles clay may tell the onlooker much about his emotional growth or about the stage he has reached in manual dexterity. The child can often tell us about himself through his materials when his immature vocabulary limits his powers of verbal expression, and in helping the child to develop his creative gifts we are helping him in his total development.

11

The nature of inspiration

In a hall were displayed paintings produced by class groups of young children of the same age working under similar conditions. Whilst all the pictures were lively and colourful, obviously painted by children in a happy classroom environment and using materials in good condition, one set of pictures was outstanding and displayed a vitality the other pictures lacked. Why is it that some teachers encourage a gifted response from the children they teach? What is it in the relationship between children and teacher that makes the difference between satisfactory and inspired work?

Inspiration is not confined to artistic pursuits, it is evident in every aspect of work in the classroom—in the way children go about their work, in the looks on their faces, in the whole of their attitude to what they are doing, both inside school and out.

As teachers, we should be more concerned with inspiring children than with teaching or instructing them. The capacity to inspire is not confined to the gifted few. Inspiration is not plucked from the air; it is not metaphysical. It depends on many practical issues, and it concerns every aspect of our work.

Each one of us has experienced, if only rarely, a state of inspiration. In such a moment we feel lifted above the level at which we normally live. In a burst of perception we are given the power to excel ourselves. We become fully aware of our own creative ability and feel capable of producing evidence of this transcendent experience. This evidence may be expressed through materials or as thought or as an imaginative solution to a problem. We recognise such experience of inspiration as a release of power which comes from within ourselves, and its release as the culmination of effort we have exerted.

'Inspiration,' says Tolstoy, 'is that which suddenly reveals what one is capable of accomplishing. The stronger the inspiration, the greater pains must be taken to bring it to fulfilment.'

Confronted by a problem, we exert effort after effort in an attempt to solve it, and each failure acts as a challenge to further effort. We may give up for a while. We may sleep, and on waking the moment of insight may show us the solution. Such experience of increased perception is the outcome of effort slowly accumulated. Frustration has a part to play, and, providing it is not too severe, is an essential challenge.

Petra found a piece of scarlet silk in the make-box. She wanted to make a dress for her doll from it, but the piece of material was small and her pattern pieces would not fit in. She arranged and rearranged them a number of times without success. At tea-time she sadly packed the material and pattern away in her box, but on arriving at school the next morning she went straight to it and took out the piece. 'I know now,' she said. 'I thought how to fit them in. If I turn these the other way round, I can get the skirt along the side.' She had solved her problem.

James is creating a picture. He has collected a wealth of materials which interest him and he moves them about the paper, absorbed in the rich colours and the way the shapes are related. He thinks through his fingers, until with sudden delight the idea is born and he works with purpose and enthusiasm until the pieces shape the picture in his mind.

Inspiration is infectious. A child may discover the joy of inspired work at first through wood, but his enthusiasm and increased sensitivity can spread to working in clay, or words, or sounds. Inspiration in one field can influence the approach to work in any other field.

In the classroom this heightened state of sensitivity depends largely on the atmosphere created by the teacher. It depends, too, on her ability to cultivate in the child an awareness of intrinsic values. Sources of inspiration are found in things, in ideas and in people, and the teacher is the child's link with these sources.

The teacher who feels and expresses genuine delight in the child's efforts will spur him on to excel himself. When she has taken active measures to know her children, and to ensure that all their possibilities have been catered for, she reacts to their work with an appreciation which is quite sincere. It is this sincerity to which a child responds and which encourages and inspires him. Above all, it is the teacher's own enthusiasm for life which will spark off life in the children she teaches. The teacher who is excited about life can stir the same excitement about it in children.

The teacher's own love of words, for instance, can develop a love and understanding of them in children. Words are the material of thought, of imagination and of creative ideas, and the teacher who shares her delight in words with her children can stir each child in the innermost citadel of his mind.

What does a collection of words such as this evoke in a child?

The Sea Shell

Sea Shell, Sea Shell,
Sing me a song, O please!
A song of ships and sailor-men,
Of parrots and tropical trees;
Of islands lost in the Spanish Main
Which no man ever may see again,
Of fishes and coral under the waves,
And sea-horses stabled in great green caves. . .
Sea Shell, Sea Shell,
Sing me a song, O please!

Amy Lowell.

It creates in the child a feeling for the deep, mysterious surging of the sea. It stimulates imagination with its suggestion of fabulous tropical islands and unexplored worlds under the sea, peopled with strange and exquisite life.

Music in the orchestration of the words thrills the child, and he feels with his whole body until he is moved to express what he feels. He may move with his body, making a dance; he may move with his hands, making a picture; he may move with his mind, making a poem or a story.

But the teacher has already built up in him other feelings and urges which he now calls upon to serve in his creation. In the painting corner he has enjoyed rich colours and muted shades. Peering through a microscope he has seen the bright green of cells from a blade of grass. She has helped him to become sensitive to colour and to words. She has prepared his mind for the spark and provided an atmosphere in which he feels free to respond.

Before a child can express himself he must have something to express, and there is much a teacher can do to prepare his mind and build up his inner resources. Self-expression cannot be taught, but observation and appreciation are activities which self-expression depends on, and these are the concern of the teacher.

Some children are born with an aptitude for observation and a memory for sense impressions, but most children need help in developing the use of their organs of sensation. Accurate observation and careful recording are as essential to the imagination as they are to science.

Atmosphere in the classroom does not depend on beautiful buildings or peaceful and glorious surroundings. Successful teaching of any kind depends on the establishment by the teacher of good attitudes between people and towards the work in hand. The type of response a teacher evokes in children is influenced by the material she gives them, by her own appearance and that of the classroom, and by her attitude to what children are and what they are trying to do.

At all stages of development the inner resources of a child can only be fully explored when his relationships are right. The relationship between teacher and child has nothing to do with power and domination; it is a relationship between people who give and take equally, each learning from the other. Teachers and children working together create the life of the school. Without this deep sense of communion life in school becomes sterile, and the results achieved are dull.

The teacher provides and maintains the conditions which foster creativity. She consciously plans opportunities which enable each child to discover his maximum capacity, and she prepares the ground for the moment when he is stimulated to use his faculties to the full. When he is saturated with the ideas, feelings and impressions she has given him, he will find an outlet through some form of expression. The sculptor, the painter, the mathematician and the scientist are fully aware of the hard toil which precedes their inspired moments. The feeding-in, the enthusiasm, delight and excitement of the child when he begins to respond, are all the responsibility of the teacher. What follows takes place inside the child, and she must depend on him to select and synthesise such experiences as will prepare him for the moment when the spark touches him.

12

Movement and the young child

The child moves because he must; movement is essential to life, and all living things move. The child starts to move long before he is born, and during childhood his body is rarely completely still. Even in sleep small movements take place in many parts of his body, both inside and out. Movement is, in fact, a natural process; we expect the child to move and we should be extremely worried if he didn't do so vigorously and continuously.

Intellectual development is rooted in exploration. As the child becomes increasingly mobile his environment enlarges, and his range of experience is directly related to his mobility. So important is mobility to the intellectual development of the child that every attempt is made to increase the mobility of limbless children at the earliest stages. The child who is restricted to his cot or who sits endlessly in a play-pen can learn little about the world. The child learns from what he encounters, and the wider his range of experience, the more he learns.

Movement is also the child's first means of expressing himself, and will remain a major means of communication throughout his life. Before the child acquires words he uses his body as a means of expressing his needs and his feelings. Attentive adults learn how to interpret the signs and this establishes the use of the body as a means of communication. As the child grows older, words will symbolise his thoughts, but his facial muscles and his hands, along with other parts of his body, will enlarge the meaning of the words he uses or compensate for their inadequacy. This use of movement persists in adult life. Many emotions are more adequately expressed through movement than through words, and the power to communicate through movement is an attribute of a vital personality.

Personality itself is inescapably reflected in the way people move. A person's style of movement is the key to his character, and the range in that style indicates his moods. What we think of ourselves affects the way we walk, or work, or sit. Some psychologists would say that even positions in sleep are indicative of personality. Alternatively, to assume a certain style of movement can affect the way we feel about ourselves and about life. To 'walk tall' can be a means of becoming a positive person.

Types of movement in a child are closely related to his stage of development and to the quality of his learning. We know that the baby will stand before he can walk, and crawl or sit before he can stand. We know at what stage we can expect him to achieve balance, to control his limbs even when standing on his hands, to perform complicated exercises on a piece of apparatus, or to sustain effort in a dance pattern. The development of the child's movements is one aspect of his total development, and the child's growing powers of movement are a form of continuous exploration rather than a subject that he can be taught.

The child needs, however, to understand his own powers of movement; he can learn how to extend these powers and to use them more effectively. He can learn to control and enjoy movement and to understand its function as a means of communicating, both with himself and with others. Movement both procures experience and provides a means of expressing experience, and education in the art of movement is as essential as education in thought or feeling.

The young child moves freely and rarely tries to move from one point to another by the most direct route. He abounds in energy, and vigorous activity is an experience of sheer joy in the capacity to move. Learning to control and perfect various ways of moving is natural to the child. Movement also provides him with the means of interpreting and mastering his environment.

An important means of understanding things in childhood is by identifying with the object or person under consideration. A young child doesn't merely pretend to be a car, or a train, or a bus conductor, he *becomes*, for the time being, the object or person he wishes to understand. By moving and performing like a cat, or like his father, he discovers what they are like and expresses what he feels about them.

Some spontaneous movements are common to all children. They jump up and down when excited, they crouch when afraid, they fling their arms wide when they are happy and confident. Such basic gestures and patterns of movement are natural and untaught. They symbolise emotions and so become units of language in much the same way as patterns of speech become words.

In schools, the importance of movement in the education of the child is now fully recognised. The way in which it is recognised has changed considerably during the last fifty years, and these changes reflect an increased understanding of the nature of childhood. In the early part of the century drill was a subject on the timetable. It was treated as physical exercise, thought to be essential for the healthy development of the child's body. Emotional enjoyment of drill wasn't considered altogether necessary, and the child bent and stretched with military precision because it was good for him.

The *1933 Syllabus of Physical Training for Schools* was based on the particular physical needs of children, who were trained to use their limbs and muscles and to perfect their skills. It was also considered important to work with others in teams. Competition was fundamental. The social aspects of movement were emerging, but the work was fundamentally physical and not closely associated with the emotional life of he child.

'Physical Training' gave way to 'Physical Education', and in recent years movements natural to the individual child have been used as the basis of his activities. The part played by the emotions and the use of the body as a means of expression are fully recognised. Children are encouraged to work individually and with other people, and movement is seen as an aspect of the child's total growth, as an end in itself and not merely as a means to an end. It is understood in terms of the activity of the whole organism, and movement of the physical body is visual evidence of movement of the mind and the imagination.

A group of seven-year-old children in one school seemed to be particularly wooden. They were unresponsive, lacked the ability to concentrate for any length of time, and were difficult to interest. They depended too much on the teacher and in spite of her efforts to encourage them to use initiative they persisted in asking what they were to do next and how to do it. The teacher attended a course in movement and then tried out its effects on the children. She used words and, later, percussion instruments to stimulate movement, concentrating on individual movement patterns.

For three or four weeks the results were disappointing. Then one day Teresa made a shaker by sealing together two plastic egg-cups containing tiny pebbles. She shook her instrument and began to respond to the sound with her body. Her teacher suggested that she should take her shaker to the movement lesson. Teresa's movement that morning was clearly inspired, and two other children joined her in making a dance pattern. Their enthusiasm was contagious, and the children began to work in a more vital way generally. By the end of the term they were capable of working out self-chosen patterns; they were beginning to work in pairs and the spontaneity of their responses delighted both themselves and their teacher.

The children's sense of movement continued to develop; they became more poised and confident, and these attitudes began to seep into other aspects of their work. They investigated materials with heightened interest, their span of attention increased, they worked together without friction and depended less and less on the teacher for direction. By the end of the year they were a group of vital, curious, and interested children who were using their abilities to the full.

In his earliest movements the child does three important things with his body. He bends, he stretches, and he twists, and these three basic movements provide the foundation for the full range of his skills. Once the child has learned to move on his feet he moves with ever-increasing skill from place to place. Energy, speed and balance become increasingly important components of his movement, and he must learn to control them.

In school we help the child to acquire control and to extend his range of movements. We encourage him to move in as many ways as possible and with as much skill as he is capable of acquiring. He is encouraged to understand the way in which his body moves and his own capacity for movement. He is free to discover for himself new ways of moving and of combining movements, and to invent different ways of doing the same thing, as, for instance, in seeing how many ways he can throw and catch a ball.

The introduction of apparatus helps to extend and vary the child's basic movements. The child who can walk on the floor will enjoy the added challenge of trying to walk on a bar at increasingly higher levels, and then of balancing along the bar using a hoop or a ball. The child who is allowed to explore for himself the use of apparatus will attempt only what he is capable of doing. It is when he is encouraged to compete with others or to perform beyond his natural capacity that accidents may occur. The teacher can suggest ways in which the child can improve his own movements, but it can be dangerous to encourage him to perform more difficult ones. As the child builds up a relationship with his apparatus, new movement will suggest itself to him.

Movement is not confined to large movements of the body. The child who can move with his body to create a dance is equally capable of moving with his hands to make a picture or a clay model, of moving with his mind to create a poem, or of moving with his imagination to create a dream or an idea.

As teachers we sometimes remain unaware of the degree to which movement is essential in learning. If we expect the child to remain still with his body and with his tongue, we must expect his mind and his imagination to slow down too. Even as adults we find movement of the body helpful to movement of the mind. Moving a pencil helps thoughts to flow; the rhythm of walking is often helpful in solving problems; and many emotional conflicts are worked out in physical activity. Even as we sit quietly lost in thought, our eyelids may blink more vigorously as the mind becomes active, or our fingers may beat a tattoo on the arm of the chair.

Young children abound in physical energy, and this must find expression in movement. It is the child's life itself, and only by encouraging the child to move in every way possible can we help him to use the life with which he is endowed.

13

The language of movement

All parts of the body move, and movement goes on in the body all the time. It is, in fact, impossible to remain completely still except in death, since movement and life are so inextricably related. Even in sleep the limbs and smaller muscles are active, and a sleeper changes position frequently; activity inside the body is continuous, the organs which maintain life never stop work and each cell of the body is in a whirl of perpetual activity, which persists even after death.

From his earliest hours the child explores his body's capacity for movement. This form of exploration is often one of pure fun, but it is also the child's main channel for his emotions. His feelings spill out through the movements of his body, and this remains his best way of expressing them until he has acquired words.

As a result of exploration the child builds up an image of his own body, and this provides him with a means of orientating himself in space. He relates to himself the objects and people around him and perceives the spaces between them and him. It is in this way that he acquires a sense of direction and of the disposition of spaces round him.

As the child acquires skill and control he becomes aware of the ways in which his movements can vary. Each movement can differ in speed, weight and fluency. Such variations in movement are associated with moods and feelings and the onlooker has little difficulty in interpreting the child's emotions. The movements of a happy, confident child contrast sharply with those of a child who feels threatened.

As adults we have learned to move with our minds and our tongues, and bodily movement as a means of expression is half-forgotten. Some teachers of young children find that moving with the child helps to reawaken a dormant means of communication, and this kinaesthetic sympathy with the child enables these teachers to feel with the child through physical forms of communication.

The movements of young children tend to be quick rather than slow and sudden rather than sustained. It requires the control of mature muscles to perform smooth, sustained, slow movements. In other words, the movements of a child are as immature as he is, and his natural ways of moving should be encouraged. The quality of his movement in later life depends on our full recognition of his natural ways of moving at each stage in his physical development. Training a young child to perform the sophisticated steps of ballet too soon can destroy the skill of a possibly gifted dancer. Fond mothers whose tiny children perform in concerts are denying their children the opportunity to live, in the fullest possible sense of the word, as children. They might just as well put them in high-heeled shoes as soon as they start to toddle.

There is much the adult can do for the child in helping him to understand the way in which his body moves, the factors involved, and their vocabulary. Children need to explore consciously their feelings of strength and lightness, of suddenness and sustainment, of variations in direction, and of all the qualities which make up human activity. They need to become aware of the partnership between emotion and movement, and of how patterns of movement can develop into dance. They need to learn through their bodies the vocabulary of movement, and to explore its possibilities as a means of communication.

The name of Rudolf Laban is associated with expressive movement, and the approaches he advocates have been developed in many Primary Schools in this country. There is a vast difference between creative work which stems from the child's natural exploration and the superimposed ideas of the teacher who suggests, for instance, that children shall become 'giants and fairies'. Laban's approach is creative and is based on the exploration of movement natural to the body. It is seen in terms of time and weight, and as taking place in space.

Movement of any kind takes time, and the length of time depends on whether the movement is fast or slow. Once a young child has acquired skill and muscular control he tends to move quickly rather than slowly, but he can associate meaning with such words as 'hurry', 'quick', 'fast', 'drag', and 'slow'. At this stage he understands the differences in these words in terms of contrast and sudden changes in time. As his movements mature, he will discriminate between various speeds more readily, and will learn how to increase or decrease speed gradually.

The young child will also understand the concept of weight in terms of contrast. He can stamp or tiptoe, punch or kick, flutter or float. He knows such words as 'strong', 'hard', 'firm', 'gentle' and 'light', and he can interpret these words through the way in which he moves.

Understanding of time and weight helps the child to know *how* to move, but he also knows something about *where* he moves. From the moment of birth the child has been learning to orientate his body in space. He learns that he can move in many directions: up and down, from side to side, backwards and forwards, round and round, and in straight or curving directions. He knows he has space all round him and that he can use it in every direction. Modern children are familiar with objects moving in many ways; they know such words as 'behind', 'sideways', 'straight', 'zig-zag' and 'twisted'. They know that each part of the body can move in a different direction and that, by so doing, the body takes on different shapes. Children of five can make themselves 'curled' or 'star-shaped', 'stretched' or 'narrow', 'big' or 'small', 'twisty' or 'spiky'.

Although children move freely in space as they play out of doors or in the house, teachers often find that in school they find space a problem. Liberated in a large hall they run round in a circle, and they are more likely to focus their movements in the direction of the teacher than to work independently of her. One of the teacher's first problems is to encourage the children to explore all available space, and to find spaces of their own away from everyone else. Encouraging each child to take an interest in getting from one place to another and to do this in as many ways as possible will help him to plan his movements independently.

In the early stages of movement education, words are the most effective means of stimulating the child to move. He knows words which denote the various parts of his body, and by associating a body word with a movement word the teacher suggests what to move and how to move it: for instance, 'Lift an elbow quickly', 'Run with your knees as high as you can', 'Move your head round and round slowly'.

Many words used to stimulate movement will acquire fresh meanings. 'Slap' can mean many things ranging between 'tap' and 'thump'; the meaning of 'lift' ranges from 'jerk' to 'lever'; 'quick' can be like the staccato patter of rain, or the flash of lightning, or the flight of birds. In this way movement adds quality to the child's vocabulary.

Movement has its own language, and it can also partner many other forms of expression and communication. It can activate the imagination, evoke as well as express a mood, stimulate creative energy and harmonise relationships between people. For action stimulates reaction, and once the child has gained confidence in his own movements he needs to exchange his movements with a partner or with a group of people.

Drama, dance, mime and pageantry all stem from movement. Craft work, painting, music-making and so on are the outcome of the partnership between a person and his materials, and movement is an essential aspect of this partnership.

Towards Christmas time, a group of children were painting pictures. One of the children painted a picture of the crib surrounded by a pop group, complete with guitars and an xylophone. 'It's the Beatles', the painter explained. 'They've come to sing to baby Jesus. They're making him a song.' Other children in the group gathered to discuss the picture appreciatively, supplementing their meagre vocabularies with gesture, mime and singing. Gradually the painting was forgotten and the children brought the Nativity to life, expressing in movement the story of how the Beatles found the baby and played all their best tunes for Him. The dance was repeated again and again and each performance was a fresh development, yet no one spoke or explained how the dance should work out. The children were communicating entirely through bodily movement, and the little group worked in complete harmony.

Words are only one means of stimulating movement. Sounds of many kinds can evoke moods, stir the emotions and the imagination, or conjure up an image which provides the idea for a dance pattern. Many of the most interesting sounds can be found in the kitchen; saucepan lids suspended on loops of string and struck with a wooden spoon produce wonderful 'gong' sounds. A wooden clothes-horse makes a good frame from which to suspend many sound-producing objects – a selection of cups and jugs, a row of orange-juice bottles containing varying amounts of water, plant-pots with rope knotted and passed through the holes in the bases, lids and pans, a triangle, lengths of wood and hollow copper-piping of different lengths.

Sometimes a child will select a percussion instrument and dance with it, or inspire a group of friends to dance as the

Senses and sensitivity

sounds suggest. Sometimes two children, working together with contrasting instruments, will weave a pattern of movements which synchronise, like the sharp staccato of castanettes and the sustained note of a chime-bar. The chinking of coins in a bag, the tinkling tune of a musical-box, sand shaken in a cardboard container: experimentation will reveal many exciting starting points for individual, partner and group work in movement.

Rhythmic patterns of sound and music offer more complicated suggestions for movement patterns. The music of the human voice is an excellent stimulant of human movement and often accompanies it. Rhymes, jingles, nursery rhymes and poetry can stir the emotions or evoke mental images which can be interpreted most readily through movement.

Sometimes a story, an idea, or an object stimulates expressive movement. Any sensory experience, such as the feel of silk or sandpaper, the sight of a windmill in full sail , the sound of the wind or of a child sobbing, even the scent of honeysuckle or the acid taste of lemon, can spark off creative dance movement.

A group of little girls were playing on tricycles along the drive. One child suggested, 'Let's make a barrier with soil and see who can run over it'. Soil from the neighbouring garden was piled across the drive. But many things lived and moved in the soil, and Madeline became absorbed in the scuttling activities of a beetle. 'Ugh!', she exclaimed, and began to wriggle; 'I'm a worm,' echoed Peta, and she curved her way in and out of Madeline's movements. Jean stood still. 'I'm a tree,' she decided, 'and you are in the soil round my roots.' She then began to sway: 'It's a bit windy,' she explained, 'there's a breeze and it's going to rain.' Julie took up the idea of rain, and when she pattered round Jean Madeline and Peta searched for shelter.

The tricycles were forgotten, and the indefinite patterns of movement began to take on form. The little drama was repeated a number of times and eventually became 'The

94

Garden Dance'. Throughout the months of summer 'The Garden Dance' remained a favourite game, to which each fresh development in the garden added a new dimension. The discovery of a pod of peas swollen to maturity, of a bee taking honey from an antirrhinum flower, of the pampas grasses rustling in the wind, all provided fresh material to weave into the dance pattern. These little girls relived, through their own movement, their observation of the ever-changing garden.

Man has always recognised the significance of movement in his life. Tribal dances stir the warrior to a frenzy of aggressive activity, they honour his wedding ceremonies, they propitiate his gods. Dance both expresses and creates a mood. Young children use movement as a natural means of expressing themselves and of exchanging experiences with other people. For them it is a wonderfully flexible form of language, and as teachers we do well to develop and retain in the child what is for him the most expressive of his skills.

14

The nature of rhythm and pulse

Rhythm is part of the nature of the child. A child's love of rhythm may be expressed in beating a drum, but beating a drum doesn't teach a child rhythm, since rhythm doesn't need to be taught; it exists in the child as part of his life. This natural love can be encouraged and deepened; it cannot be imposed.

The child's first experience of rhythm is pre-natal. The developing embryo rests near its mother's heart, which beats in a rhythmic pattern. Via the placenta, maternal blood carries food, oxygen and water to be absorbed by the blood of the embryo, and in return waste products are transferred to the mother's blood. Long before it is born, the baby therefore depends on the rhythmic activity of his mother's body for life. This living rhythm persists in his own body after birth has made him an independent organism. Only at death will this rhythmic activity cease.

These patterns of living rhythm exist not only within the child himself but are fundamental to the environment which surrounds him. The rhythm of night and day, of the seasons and the tides, of the life-cycles of plants and insects, the rhythm of swaying grass and flowing river, the chewing of cows as they graze, the humming of bees or the sound of crickets vibrating their limbs, these and many other forms of rhythm impinge on the child. Without them life would not exist.

While every child has rhythm, this varies from child to child. Young children need to explore individual rhythm before they can enjoy a rhythm common to a group, and they often find it difficult to keep 'in time' with music. Before moving to music they need ample opportunity to move freely in a large space.

Visual evidence of the child's sense of rhythm can be observed from his earliest days. The baby sucking at his mother's breast has his own rhythmic pattern. By the time he is twelve months old he can bang an uneven rhythm with his spoon on a tray, and he makes explosive sounds with his lips in bursts of rhythmic pattern. A two-year-old can bounce up and down on his father's knee, he loves the swings on the park or the rhythmic movement of Grannie's rocking-chair. Bodily response to his innate feeling of rhythm will persist, and with help it can develop and bring the child great joy and satisfaction. Undeveloped, it remains in adult life an unexplored sensory pleasure and may only be discharged through the fingers or toes as they echo the rhythm of an orchestra.

Whilst most adults sense the significance of rhythm, few can accept the rhythmic pattern of life. The fact that joy and sorrow, success and adversity, love and hate, are complementary aspects of this pattern evades them, and they complain when life brings them unpleasant as well as pleasant experience. They aspire to live perpetually in the heights, unaware that in order to do this one must experience the depths. They want to live half of life, not all of it, because they fail to appreciate the whole of its rhythmic pattern.

Young children must have the opportunity to experience living rhythm in all its diversity, and those in charge of young children must help them to explore and to use their innate sense of rhythm, harmony and balance. Space and time are the fundamental elements of rhythm, and it is through his own body that the child grows to understand the inseparable partnership of the two. Music enables the child to discover this rhythmic unity, which he will find in many other aspects of art. The child who can move rhythmically with his body can weave patterns with paint on paper, can shape his thoughts in rhythmic patterns of words or create a garden in a rhythm of soil, rocks and plants.

Rhythm is closely related to balance and symmetry, and most rhythmic experiences include the property of balance. The child on a see-saw learns the significance of equality, and he develops this sense of equilibrium when he explores equipment for weighing or when he spins the globe on its axis. He learns the law of compensation; what is taken out must be repaid, when he is tired he must rest, when he is hungry he must eat. He discovers the essential need of the body to remain in balance, and later he comes to recognise the necessity of a balanced mind.

So important is balance to man that many religious beliefs incorporate the concept, in particular that point of balance where there is absolutely no movement. T. S. Eliot in his *Four Quartets* speaks of it as 'the still point', the 'timeless moment', and 'the point of intersection of the timeless with time'. This centre is interpreted as the point of contact between man and belief, and the human being who reaches it is said to be transformed and integrated.

The ideal state of mental health is complete harmony within the human organism. Man spends his life striving towards this sense of total balance. It is never fully achieved, though it may be experienced for fleeting moments, but it is the lodestar which directs man's life and gives him a reason for living. Quakers begin each of their meetings with a conscious attempt to 'centre down' and to create contact for a channel of communication among members of the group and between each person's 'inner light' and 'that of God in every man'. In the third century St. Isaak of Syria said, 'Endeavour to enter your own inner cell, and you will see the heavens, because the one and the other are one and the same, and when you enter one you see the two.' This idea has remained basic to religious belief, and it emphasises the significance of inner peace and complete mental balance.

The principles of exploration apply as much to movement as to the use of any other creative material. The young child uses his own experiences and emotions when he starts to explore the movement of his body, and he needs first the freedom to discover his own body and the way in which he can use it before he is ready to organise his discoveries and to use movement as a means of expressing himself. Expression and communication are not the same process, however, and it may be some time before the child is ready to work with a partner or in a group.

Although emotions often result in movement, it may be quite a long time before the child associates the two. He may be six or seven before he is consciously aware that crouching expresses fear or that leaping expresses joy. Gradually he will build up a memory of his own movements until he has a vocabulary of movement symbols which he can use in communicating with others. He is then ready to interpret the movements of other children and to respond in articulate ways, and only then will he be interested in working with a partner or in weaving a pattern of dance in a group.

An interesting experiment was carried out by the headmistress of one school. She was anxious to explore the possibilities of movement with the children in her school, and she established the idea of a voluntary movement session. Children from any part of the school, with an age range of four-and-a-half to eleven, could join in.

For many, even of the older children, this was their first experience of creative dance, and in the first weeks each child needed to go through the initial stages of exploration. The ideas of body awareness were new to them, and they had to learn from scratch the vocabulary of their own body movement. Ten-year-old children worked alongside the five-year-olds in an independent and self-centred fashion.

After about three or four sessions some of the older children began to work in pairs. Sharing a space increased the interest, and responding to the initiative of another child added a sense of adventure to dance. At the end of the fifth period, a group of nine- and ten-year-olds approached the headmistress. 'We like to come with the little ones,' they explained, 'but can we have an advanced class as well? We want to make a sort of picture and the little ones don't know what we are doing.' Their advanced class was established and the children developed ideas from pictures of Greek friezes they had found in a book. They worked as a group or sometimes in pairs and reserved the earlier part of the lesson to 'practise our shapes'.

These children had rediscovered the idea of dance as a basic means of communication. They were ready to understand the significance of tribal dance, and the headmistress told them about the ritual dances of African tribes, performed before hunting expeditions. The children were fired by the idea of evoking excitement and the zest for chase by dance, so they evolved ritual dances of their own and were able to experience the elemental power of movement. The study of life in Africa which stemmed from this incident was a vivid and vital piece of learning. Never had a geographical study had such quality.

Teachers can quote many examples of the way in which the child's developing skill in movement can affect other aspects of his work. Glenda aged seven was an intelligent child, but her gifts were of an academic kind and creative work held little interest for her. Although her teacher had provided an inspiring collection of fabrics and other materials for picture-making, Glenda made no attempt to create a picture. Sometimes she fingered the pieces of velvet and cotton appreciatively, but they failed to stimulate in her an urge to use them.

One day a gossamer-fine remnant of pink georgette filled

her with delight. She lifted it, swirling it around, and then let it fall gently to the ground. She repeated the movement, and her body echoed the movement of the silk. She danced with her georgette, round and round the classroom and into the hall beyond. The movement of the silk was dominated by Glenda's own rhythm as the two developed a partnership of rhythmic pattern.

For some time Glenda remained absorbed by her dance; then she returned to the fabric box and selected many pieces of lightweight material. She took silk and nylon, net and organza, feathers and a snippet of swansdown and some lengths of angora wool. She laid a large sheet of thin cardboard on the floor and let her scraps of material float down onto it, and then pasted them to the card with minute spots of gum. A bodily response to her materials had induced her to create her first picture.

The quality of such experiences depends on their nearness to the child's own nature. Dance, which holds living pulse at its heart, is a form of creative energy which can inspire the child. The monotony of mechanical beat can deaden this energy. It produces repetitive patterns of sound in music and lifeless responses in movement. Pulse, on the other hand, is at the heart of movement. The freedom and grace of a gifted dancer stems from her ability to use the living pulse as a source of inspiration. Beating out a pattern of sound can pin a child down to a dance which is merely repetitive, but giving the child the opportunity to explore his own sense of pulse leaves him free to weave a throbbing pattern of natural rhythm as he moves.

Beat and pulse are elements of rhythm. Pulse is related to the throbbing of the heart and is the vibrating heart of movement. It should not be confused with beat, which is a repeated strike, used to mark time in music. Sometimes teachers beat on a drum or a tambourine in the belief that this represents rhythm. They may even give each child a percussion instrument and set one child to beat out a pattern of sound, either with an instrument or with a baton. The rigid and monotonous pattern of sound which often results from this procedure they may call music, or rhythmic accompaniment, when in fact the living beat or pulse has been destroyed by mechanical repetition of sounds. There is a world of difference between a tattoo and the pulsation of the human heart. Producers of films on television know this and the recorded sound of the human heart is frequently used to inspire fear and deep emotion, when the tattoo of a drum beat would reduce the same scene to comedy.

Teachers can most help the child by giving him the opportunity to discover and use the pulse of his own life.

15

Making music

When the leaves of a tree hang still they are silent, but when
the wind ruffles them they move and sound is produced. The
link between vibration and sound remains a constant element
of music, and children who have learned to understand movement have the foundation for an understanding of music.

A tune or a song can be quick or slow, and we have a wide
vocabulary of terms with which to express the possible
variations in speed, from 'prestissimo' (very quick) to 'largo'
(slow). Children of six and seven can appreciate increase and
decrease in speed, and through their own bodily movement
they can understand the meaning of the words 'accelerando'
(with increasing speed) or 'ritardando' (with diminishing
speed); but while many children enjoy knowing and using
these terms, expressions such as 'speed up' or 'slow down'
would be more meaningful for some.

Music can be loud or soft, powerful and strong or gentle and
light; and children can associate heavy steps or punching with
strong music, and flicking fingers or tiptoeing with light
music. To the young child both time and weight in music are
understood in terms of contrast, and he may be nine or ten
before he can discriminate between the finer qualities of sound.

In music there are high notes and low notes, and many
children stand on their toes when trying to sing high notes

or sink their chins into their chests when singing low ones. The term 'pitch' may present some difficulties to the child, and he may be able to recognise it in a melodic percussion instrument before he can tell you whether he is himself singing high or low.

The combination of music and movement is natural to children. Timothy, aged eighteen months, bangs his heels on the floor to the accompaniment of explosive sounds produced by his lips. Jennifer, at the age of four, jumps up and down on the spot as she sings, 'I'm Jennifer Tomlinson ... I'm Jennifer Tomlinson ...', and when she hears orchestral music she sways and swirls to express her response to it.

Music can be an incentive to dance. It can evoke a mood, conjour an image, or suggest a way of moving. However, it does not 'tell you what to do', as many teachers think who play a record and tell the children to 'move to the music' or 'do what the music says'. Sometimes the child will try to match his movements to the sound he hears. At other times he may weave a pattern of dance which expresses the mood or ideas stimulated by the music. More often than not the very young child simply moves while the record plays on, and what he is doing may be quite unrelated to the sound he hears. Even at later stages of development music should never dominate movement, for movement and sound are partners, and harmony cannot exist between them if either dominates.

The exploration of sound itself is often the starting point of an interest in musical composition, and sound plays a very important part in the child's life from his earliest days. One of the few things which frighten a baby is a loud or sudden noise. He may cry if he hears his mother's voice raised in anger, even though she is not angry with him. A baby of a few days old responds to the human voice. When his mother speaks or sings her mouth fascinates him, and when he is a bit older he may try to pluck it from her face. As he discovers his ability to make vocal sounds he revels in the delight of making his own noises, and he amuses himself for hours by babbling and other forms of pre-speech play. Once he discovers the thrill of banging, clattering and scraping, his joy is boundless, and very soon his sounds will begin to take on rhythmic form.

Meanwhile the child is growing increasingly aware of the wealth of sounds which surround him. Soon he begins to discriminate between those he likes and those he does not. His choice is largely individual and is usually emotionally based. If he enjoys his bath he learns to love the sound of running water. If a dog has previously frightened him he will cry when he hears one bark. Some sounds are universal in their appeal, and most of these are musical and have rhythm.

The child's own voice remains his most pleasurable source of music-making, and he enjoys imitating and singing songs, rhymes and jingles. Many children of three or four can imitate and memorise tunes which they hear repeated on radio and on records. But the greatest pleasure of all comes from the exploration of the possibilities of the child's own voice.

Alison loved the sounds of words. She repeated a word which interested her, irrespective of whether she knew its meaning or not, and she could intone it in a variety of ways. Such words as 'merry-go-round', 'elephant', 'cellophane' and 'violin' were part of her repertoire. Often she sat at the piano playing imaginary tunes as she sang her songs. Sometimes her little voice seemed to emulate different instruments. She loved the wind and to dance along a windswept beach, her voice competing with the sounds of the wind and the waves.

The ways in which children can explore the properties and behaviour of sound are described in the third book in this series. Knowledge and understanding of sound help children to appreciate the musical use of sound. Indeed, musical composition is often the outcome of scientific exploration and experimentation, just as many home-made musical instruments start as experiments in shaking, tapping or plucking.

A number of excellent books of instructions for making

musical instruments have already been published. Children can be encouraged to experiment with many kinds of objects and materials for making musical sounds. One small 'orchestra' employed the following instruments: a zip-fastener, a damp cork rubbed on glass, a roller on thick paint, rubber bands, a tube of chocolate beans, an egg whisk and a length of stiff silk.

Exploring a real musical instrument is part of the child's musical education. Too often children are 'taught' to play the piano before they have had the opportunity to explore various ways of producing sounds from it. Some local authorities now supply schools with discarded pianos so that children can make these discoveries for themselves. Systematic tuition is essential at some stage if the child is to master the techniques of any instrument, but teaching technique before the child has built up his own relationship with an instrument is largely a waste of time and may turn the child against playing it. Many children have been turned against the piano for ever by an over-enthusiastic 'instructor' in their early days.

Simple instruments which enable a child to play tunes should be available at every stage. The days when the child's contribution was to keep time with a percussion instrument while the teacher played the tune have gone, and we now recognise the need for the child to make his own music. Perhaps the most versatile of such instruments are chime-bars, xylophones, or glockenspiels. Again, children left free to explore these instruments handle them with confidence, and they make original tunes in addition to imitating tunes they know.

When Elizabeth was first introduced to the chime-bars she preferred to handle them one at a time. She described her notes in different ways: 'A' she called 'my far-away tune', 'G' was 'the strong tune', and 'C' 'the home tune'. Eventually she placed her chime-bars at random in a row and tapped them to see what tune they made. She then retained some of the sequences which pleased her and repeated them. Later she put some of these sequences together and made the following tune:

'A Slow Tune'

The pentatonic harp is a simple and delightful instrument. It has five notes (C, D, E, G and A), and any combination of these notes produces harmony. By plucking it the child gains a sense of playing a piece of music, even though he knows nothing about harmony and composition. At the same time his ear becomes accustomed to a harmonious combination of notes.

Sometimes a familiar song or tune is used as the foundation of original work. One group of seven-year-old children adopted the tune 'Three Blind Mice', using a recorder, a glockenspiel, a set of tubular-chimes and a tambourine. The tubular-chimes maintained the original tune, while the other instruments improvised on the basic theme. The result was highly amusing – a piece of music with many variations.

Sometimes tune and dance are created together. On one occasion the weather was thundery, and spectacular clouds banked the sky. Lightning flickered behind the clouds and huge raindrops plopped one at a time on the paving stones beyond the classroom window. Roy, aged six-and-a-half, fetched a gong-drum and beat out a muffled rhythm, singing, 'I'm thunder... I'm thunder...' Other children huddled together to represent the clouds, some of them swaying about near the ground while others hovered menacingly above. The threatening cloud mass heaved and rolled across the room, while Roy continued to intone, 'Soon it will lighten. The lightning... the lightning... the lightning dances through the cloud and raindrops rush down, down, down onto the ground.'

The little dance drama lasted for about five minutes, until a torrent of rain-drops against the window-pane reminded the children of the real storm outside. The dance was not repeated. It existed only as an expression of mood created by the thunderstorm, and as the mood passed, so did the dance.

The whole purpose of music is to give pleasure. The child's natural love of it shows that he delights in it, and this love should never be dissipated. There is no point in having the child memorise a song or in teaching him to play a piece of music on the piano or violin if he is forced beyond his pace, for the exercise then becomes drudgery.

It is through his attempts to compose his own tunes or by playing a 'concerted' arrangement of a nursery rhyme or song that the child learns to appreciate the music-making of others. His own humble experiments with chime-bars or recorder can help him to become sensitive to the creative genius of Mozart and Bach. His understanding of music will come to him through his own struggles with movement and sound.

16

Appreciating the music-making of others

Much as children enjoy making their own music even the youngest child can find added pleasure in the music made by others. A mother makes music for her baby naturally, by singing to him, and few mothers would question their ability to do this. Many mothers recognise the interest of the young child in music, which is used to soothe and calm the baby and also to give him positive pleasure.

Musical talent develops very early in childhood and it is in their early years that children need ample opportunity to develop sensitivity to and understanding of music. We can help them to do this by making music a very active part of the child's environment. Unfortunately, however, in many schools music tends to be regarded as a pleasurable addition to the programme rather than as an integral part of the child's education. Teachers feel inadequate, and while, as non-specialists, primary school teachers will tackle most other aspects of education with confidence, they have the mistaken idea that only the gifted musician can teach music. Even in schools which run an otherwise integrated programme a musically talented member of staff or even a visiting specialist teaches music as a separate subject.

Fortunately most colleges now expect all students training as primary teachers to take music as a professional course, and very often each student must learn to play an instrument. They are given definite help in selecting and introducing music to children, and many 'non-musical' students discover unexpected talents and pleasure in music as a result of these courses.

There is available to children as rich a heritage and tradition of music as there is of literature. The teacher who can give the child access to this store of material need be neither a musician nor an expert musical critic. If she has developed her own enjoyment of music and has taken the trouble to acquaint herself with the material available she is perfectly capable of helping the child to become appreciative of good music and to become musically literate.

The child's world of today abounds in harsh sound and noise, and the capacity to listen needs careful cultivation if it is to remain a source of pleasure in adult life. Young children are still learning how to hear. What they hear and how they listen as young children will instil in them listening habits which will persist in adult life. If they hear nothing but shrieking voices and the clatter of machinery and traffic, musical sounds will be strange and unfamiliar. If they are brought up in homes where orchestral music from the television set perpetually competes with the conflicting noises of a cluttered and disorganised home, they will not learn how to listen when they hear music outside the home. They will adopt the attitude of their parents to music and will acquire the habit of switching it off as if it were an interruption.

It is while the child is still learning to hear that adults can help him to make his hearing grow into listening. Being listened to is part of learning to listen, and the adult who listens to the child as he chatters or sings or makes music is an educational asset.

In the early stages the child's span of listening attention may be short. As he learns how to listen and to make his listening creative his attention increases, and many children of eight or nine are capable of enjoying an orchestral concert. It is quite untrue to say that children of this age cannot concentrate for any length of time. One teacher who took a group of six- to nine-year-old children to a Hallé Concert found that their rapt absorption was much deeper than that of many of the rustling and coughing adults nearby.

A reasonably quiet room is essential for listening to music. There are many ways in which we can bring music to children. The teacher herself can sing or play to them, and most of the traditional songs, nursery rhymes and folk songs are introduced to children in this way. The radio and record-player are aids which enable the teacher to introduce the child to a wide variety of music. Many teachers are becoming increasingly skilful in using the tape-recorder, and can thus collect suitable music from a number of sources to add to their musical library. Many publishing companies specially prepare lists of good music for the young listener, and suggestions for suitable music for listening will be found in Appendix 3 of this book.

Although children enjoy short spells of direct listening, much of what they hear is intimately bound up in other aspects of their daily experience. Music forms part of the school service, of the dramatic play of the child, of his movement experience, of his interest in foreign countries or of people in history, of his scientific observation of sound, or of his work with creative materials. The following examples will show how some teachers have enriched the activities of children by including music.

A group of children had returned to school after their summer vacation. Following from their initial experiences of holiday beaches their teacher urged them, metaphorically, to adventure across the ocean. Some became absorbed in ways of crossing the sea, while others explored deep-sea diving and were particularly interested in marine life. The aquarium music for Saint-Saën's 'Carnival of the Animals' was introduced to them by their teacher, and the listeners were taken deeper into their imaginary world, peopling an ocean with strange and exotic fish. The pictures they made later reflected the impact of this experience.

Children who worked in a school not far from the River Trent wanted to know where the water came from. As a result of their enquiry they were taken by their teacher to a hillside in Derbyshire, where they saw the spring which was said to be the source of the river. The children could scarcely believe that such a tiny stream could be the beginning of so great a river. Many of them still clung to their belief that the Trent existed beneath Trent Bridge and not much further.

Their teacher then played them the 'Vltava' music by Smetana and told them the story of the river which rose in the heart of a great forest from two springs, one warm and one cold, and after passing through a big city joined a second river, growing deeper and wider and sometimes broken by a waterfall. The beauty and majesty of the 'Vltava' music conveyed an impression of the vast river and of the way in which it flowed for many miles. It carried the children along on its swelling stream, and they were able to transfer these images to their own river. Their revised concept of the Trent was far more accurate than anything a picture or even a film could have inspired. The river music was used frequently during the school service and the children came to regard it as 'our own river music'.

The teacher's selection of music depends considerably on her own taste. What she enjoys the children will also. If she is unsure about the works of some of the modern composers, she can explore them with the children. The rhythm and colour of certain modern works appeal to children, and many teachers find that their own pleasure grows as a result of exploring new ground with children. Seeing the uninhibited pleasure of the young child can break through the adult's resistance to unaccustomed combinations of sound.

Some authorities employ pianists who visit schools for perhaps one or two sessions a week. Even the Infant School is expected to use the pianist, although her intermittent appearance may seem to be an interruption to a continuous programme. Often these pianists are good instrumentalists and have a wealth of information about music and composers, and there is no reason why children should be assembled in a large group to sing merely because a pianist has been paid to visit the school, nor is there any reason why she should be employed to play for a movement session. Indeed, many movement sessions may need the pianist only briefly.

Such activities are not very satisfactory expenditures of a pianist's time, for these specialists can add considerably to the musical education of the children if they are properly used. In one school groups of children awaited the visit of the pianist with great pleasure because she told them stories about Handel and Mozart and illustrated her stories with short extracts from their works. Sometimes she played music from India or China, and since there were a number of immigrants in the school she encouraged them to sing to the other children.

Among the parents attached to any school will be found a number of musicians. It may be big brother with his pop group, or 'Grandad who plays the violin in the Albert Hall', or mother who plays the harp in the local orchestra. These specialists can be persuaded to visit the school, perhaps for the service or during a spring festival or Christmas carol service. They are part of the child's adult environment and add to his musical experience.

Learning to read music is no more difficult than learning to read words or the positions of the hands on the clock. Some children learn to read staff notation from their attempts to record their own music. A flannelgraph, on which the children can place notes in position, is inexpensive to make or to purchase. The work of Carl Orff shows how language and music are related; and in some Infant Schools children can both compose and write out their own tunes and songs, and read from a musical score. In a few schools sol-fa work is used in singing, and children can write out and play tunes they have made by recording them in sol-fa.

The world outside school abounds in musical opportunity. The teacher can help the child to notice, use and appreciate much that reaches him by radio, television and record-player in the home. Many children nowadays have record-players of their own, but their record-collections may suffer from the influence of adults. With help and encouragement from the teacher they can add to their collections such records as 'The Sorcerer's Apprentice' by Dukas, or 'Peter and the Wolf' by Prokofiev, which the children may have heard during the school service or movement lesson. Likewise the teacher can help the child to be selective in his listening to television or transistor. Some children enjoy opera, or they may grow to love music through watching ballet. The parents of one nine-year-old were surprised and delighted when they took him to see his first ballet performance, and he told them, 'I don't need to read what it says on the programme. I know the story and the music. We had it in school with our headmaster.' He sat enthralled through the performance of the one-act version of 'Swan Lake', and he was ready to extend the same attention to the unfamiliar modern ballet which followed.

As children grow older they enjoy trying to play musical instruments. Their early efforts with home-made instruments provide them with an understanding of the way in which music is made, and by the time they are nine many children are capable of playing in, for instance, a recorder group and of interpreting the music of familiar composers if it is simply arranged. In some schools the range of instruments is wider, and children of seven and upwards play violins, flutes, recorders and percussion, and the school orchestra plays a prominent part in their education. In schools such as these, children are learning to regard music as a source of inspiration and pleasure and to grow up in a world enriched for them by their own music-making as well as by the music-making of others.

17

The body as an instrument

An instrument in itself has little meaning. It can only fulfil its purpose when it is being used. A violin requires a player before it can produce music, and the quality of music produced depends as much on the player as on the instrument. This partnership between operator and instrument is fundamental, and within that partnership something is created which could not exist outside of it.

Since the true purpose of an instrument is to serve as a means towards an end, the value of that instrument depends on whether it can do this economically and efficiently. However, it is the quality brought to the job by the operator which determines the extent to which the possibilities of the instrument can be used. When the instrument is good it improves with use, and, providing the materials from which the instrument are made are durable, practice can bring about improvement in performance both of the player and of the tool he uses.

The most wonderful of instruments is the human body, which is a highly complicated synthesis of interdependent systems. What kind of an instrument it is and how it works depend on the person it embodies; the things the body achieves are expressions of the relationship between the person and his body.

Each man in characterised by his outward appearance, and the shape of his body, the expression on his face and the way his body moves describe the qualities of the man and his attitudes to life. Even the style of the body has changed with the times: modern man bears little resemblance to his pugilistic, hunting forefathers, and people who live in steamy forests are of a different type from those who live in cars and centrally-heated buildings.

Perhaps the most eloquent part of the human body is the face. The shape of the mouth and the lines which surround it are fashioned by the habits of the muscles which control it. How these muscles behave is governed by the mind. Even the child, whose experience of life is only that of a few years, expresses in his face what he habitually feels, his degree of intelligence and the attitude he has towards other people. In the face of an adult we can decipher his intellect, his habits, virtues and vices, and his general sense of responsibility with regard to his role in life. Harmony in the human face has a beauty which persists irrespective of age and the ravages of experience, and this harmony comes from the spirit of the man behind the face.

What the body becomes as it develops is largely dependent on how it moves. If the body remained perfectly still it would not, of course, develop at all. Movement and development are inextricably dependent on one another, and we must first consider what it is that makes the body move at all.

The need to survive exists in man at birth and much of his early activity stems from his attempts to satisfy the needs of the body and his efforts to educate it to become independent. The baby struggles towards a life which frees him of his parents and others on whom he depends, although in order to exist he must be nourished and protected.

At first someone sees to these things for him, but his future as a person is assured only by his ability to dispense with too great a degree of dependence on others. This urge motivates him to action, and the satisfaction which such activity brings him helps to establish in him a permanent pattern of activity. Sometimes adults regard inactivity on the part of the child as a virtue, but the 'good' child, or one who doesn't disturb the adult, is one who makes little effort to explore his environment or to use his body. Over-protective adults also rob the child of the incentive to fend for himself, and consequently they rob him of his opportunity to develop.

Even the most perfect body needs activating if it is to live. When we come to examine the causes for its activity we become aware that outward stimuli are ineffective unless the organism responds with its internal energies. Some of these responses may be said to be automatic, but the more important responses stem from individual qualities existing within the organism, which vary from person to person, causing them to respond in different ways to the same set of stimuli.

Psychologists have made a detailed study of motivation in human behaviour, and they recognise its significance in the learning situation. A few examples may indicate some of the sources of this life energy. Physiological needs dominate activity in early life. When a baby is hungry he cries and shows his distress by throwing his arms and legs about. His skin is flushed and in every part of his body he is trying to express his need, in the hope that those he depends on will come to his rescue. If he were not fed he would persist in his activity until he literally wore himself out, even to the point of death.

However, the human baby is a social being by nature. His need for the companionship and approval of others is as strong as his basic need to survive, and he learns to control his needs in order to fit in with the wishes of others. His need for social acceptance will cause him to wait patiently until his meal is served. The child's psychological and social needs may conflict with his physiological needs, but often the former are strong enough to dominate his behaviour.

If a child lacks motivation his activities remain stunted. A child who has had everything done for him at home may enter school unable to fasten his own buttons, but when he finds that he cannot go out to play until he has fastened up his own coat buttons he learns to do this very quickly.

John, at the age of nine, had never learned how to swim. He wanted to join the school camp, and when he was told that as the camp was situated on the edge of a lake only boys who could swim could go, he managed to accomplish this skill in three or four weeks.

Judith was a self-willed little girl. At home she had no companions of her own age and no idea of how to share her toys with others. When she first came to school she was possessive and often aggressive when she couldn't have her own way. However, she was also in very great need of friends to play with, and she learned to control her aggression and to share her possessions with others.

In each of these situations the body was activated by some inner drive, and in the case of Judith a braking system was also brought into action. The source of the body's energy is food, but this energy can remain unused until some drive from elsewhere within the human organism summons it into activity.

Without analysing in clinical detail the chemistry of the human body, we can underline some of the forces which serve as energisers. We know that fear can make the skin turn pale and that it can tap unexpected resources of energy when, for example, we try to run away. We know that joy produces an awakened feeling, and that what we need to do is performed with added zest when we are happy. Misery and depression, on the other hand, slow us down and make life a burden.

One of the most powerful of all energisers is what we might call inspiration, such as is provided by an idea, a person, or a situation. When we work in a state of inspiration we are shown what we are capable of doing. In such a state the body seems to become tireless as it calls upon untapped sources of energy.

The emotions, then, play an important part in the activation of the body, and when the mind and the emotions are in sympathy activity reaches its peak. The professional artist trains his body to perform well under many conditions, but even the most skilful artist has moments of inspiration in which he excels himself.

Movement of the bodily instrument can take many forms: it can move in a big way, involving the limbs and larger muscles; it can move in some single part involving perhaps the voice or the hands or the face; it can move mainly in the mind or in the imagination, and we speak of being 'moved' by an experience when, to all intents and purposes, the body remains still.

The most expressive forms of movement are rooted in the emotions. Experiences which stimulate deep feeling trigger off a chain of activity which culminates in the total or partial use of the body. What we feel can be expressed in many different ways. The body has many tunes which spring from happiness, and an expression of joy can take the form of a song or a dance, a painting or a poem. Movements of the limbs or of the hands or of the mind are equally eloquent of feeling.

In school children should feel free to move in all the ways they are capable of. Drawing a picture is not their only means of expressing their impressions of a story; writing about an exciting experiment is not the only way of recording it. The child's impressions of a rough sea can move him to use his voice in making a song, or his hands in painting a picture, or his mind and imagination in some form of creative writing, as often as he is moved to use his body in making a dance.

The child has, in his own body, a most versatile instrument and he should be encouraged to explore all its varied uses. Woodwork, pottery, drama, music, dance and mime are all activities which children can experience, not simply for the sake of achieving skill in them, but so that they can know what it feels like to do these things. The child who has met his own inadequacies in artistic work can appreciate the skill of the expert, but he is also discovering that his own body is the instrument of his education.

This is perhaps the ultimate purpose of the human body: to serve as the tool by which the personality is shaped. The teacher can nourish the child's mind and provide good opportunities for the exercise of his emotions, but it is the child's body itself which teaches him and which leads him to become the person he is. The good teacher is the one who can help the child to become fully aware of his physical person and of all it can accomplish. The child who knows his instrument well wil' play it well.

18

Unity of personality

Living involves the child in developing the relationship that exists between himself and his surroundings. He is constantly deepening his world of inner experiences as he extends his world of experiences surrounding him. Personality is the result of the interaction of the inner and outer aspects of his world, and has been described by G. W. Allport as 'an endeavour to balance inner and outer pressures in order to achieve a state of rest or equilibrium'.

One of man's deepest needs is for self-identity, that is, to be recognised as one person with an integrated personality. Only when he has achieved this can he be said to be himself, though very few people can remain themselves under all circumstances. Most of us have the chameleon's habit of playing a part which fits in with our immediate surroundings. The companion who enables us to be ourselves and to dispense with acting is a very special friend, and we love him because with him we are no longer torn apart by the many conflicting selves within our personal make-up.

There is a tendency in every living organism to maintain within itself relatively stable conditions. In the pre-natal stages regulatory mechanisms operating in the mother do this for the foetus. Once the baby is on his own his body must deal with the situation, and his life becomes a persistent search for stability. This constant endeavour to remain in balance is fundamental to physical life and to personality. It is, moreover, a total experience, and each aspect of balance within the individual affects the organism as a whole.

At the physical level examples of this search for balance are constantly operating. The body temperature is maintained by sweating and shivering, so that when the body becomes too hot perspiration helps to reduce the temperature, and shivering is an involuntary activity of the muscles to warm the body up. When tissues are injured and destroyed, white blood cells hasten to protect them. Deeper breathing helps to restore the carbon dioxide level when the air we breathe is deficient in oxygen. Sleep restores the tired body and food appeases hunger.

The development of personality is an experience of constant adjustment. It is the outcome of all an organism does in the way of living. Life could be described as a constant attempt to maintain balance between two extremities.

The human baby is helpless at birth and almost completely dependent. He immediately sets himself on the journey towards independence, and his first cry is a demand for air which will enable him to breathe independently of his mother. From that moment he directs his efforts towards becoming an independent person, a goal he will never quite reach. Survival depends on independence, and life is lived between these two extremities.

The body's fight to maintain balance is evident. Temperature, pulse-rate, heart-beat, nutrition and many other processes are kept constant. Psychological balance is equally important, and the need for emotional unity has always been recognised by philosophers and educators. Plato regarded musical training as the most powerful instrument of balance, 'because rhythm and harmony find their way into the inward places of the soul'. He felt that harmony in the soul produced harmony in the body.

Pestalozzi was essentially aware of the complete nature of the human organism, and he saw the mind of the child as a seed which held all his ultimate potential. He saw life as the unfolding of this seed and education as an experience affecting the whole man. 'Only that which affects man as an indissoluble unit is educative in our sense of the word. It must reach his hand and his heart as well as his head.'

The constant desire for harmony of the body and mind involves unification with the environment. Being at one with the world means that we must come to terms with our surroundings, and this is a two-way process. Perception and understanding of the world of external experiences bring about changes in the world of inner experiences. What we experience we try to recreate in an attempt to gain an understanding and inner vision of it.

We may move to a new house and find that instead of small windows looking out over the tops of roofs and chimneys we have large windows with a view of the garden outside. The home we make in the new house may contain much the same furniture as did our old home, but we now arrange it so that the view is unimpeded. Windows are for looking out of as well as for letting in light, and the way we plan the home expresses our changing idea of it.

Before birth the baby is unified. His mother's body ensures a state of equilibrium for him, and he is always at the right temperature, adequately nourished, and suspended in water to protect him from adverse conditions. He is in no way threatened, and his needs are met as they arise. There are no major challenges, and life is smooth and uneventful until the shattering moment of birth.

Birth is possibly the most challenging event a baby will ever experience. He is thrust from the harmonious protection of his mother's womb into a world where temperature is constantly changing, where he is cut off from his source of air and nourishment and surrounded by a confusion of stimuli he doesn't understand. He spends a lifetime working towards maturity or the unification of his personality. Prolonged immaturity extends his learning period, and this learning ranges over many situations and lasts for many years, its ultimate goal being to return him to his early state of unification.

It would be difficult to forecast the baby's future personality at birth, and yet although external circumstances will be influential, the basic pattern is already laid down, and the baby will grow towards the person only he can become. His mental health depends on his becoming that self, and neurotic behaviour is a symptom of some interference with the process of self-realisation. Inner serenity is the result of self-realisation, and it is the complete antithesis to neurosis.

It is perhaps only in rare moments that adults experience complete inner harmony, and it is doubted whether a state of permanent and complete harmony would be altogether desirable. As long as we strive we grow; complete harmony might produce a static condition. Self-realisation is manifested by the maximum use of potential. Only then are we at our best and capable of making mature relationships with others.

The development of personality and ultimate self-realisation depend on human relationships. The natural process of becoming oneself can take place only in the human situation, so that this process is subject to constant interference. Perhaps the most important circumstance is love, for full development of the person takes place only in an atmosphere of love, given and received. The child learns to love by experiencing love, and one who has had little or no experience of love in his early years is incapable of loving or of making adequate relationships. His personality becomes stunted and he has little hope of ever becoming a full person.

Parents who love their child objectively, who can love him without self-interest, provide the best possible circumstances for his satisfactory development as a person. When, in a similar way, other important adults in his life extend their love to him, his chances of self-realisation are assured. He needs to feel from the start, and then throughout life, that these adults want him to become himself, and that he is not obliged to become what they think he should be. The unfolding personality has its unique pattern, and no other person has the right to bend it to suit his own ideas.

As adults we experience this sense of unity in different ways. For one person, toiling with rocks and soil to create a garden brings a sense of inner peace; for another, it may be in the creative work of others that complete harmony is found.

So it is with children. David has chosen terracotta clay, and has formed his figure of a man, stiff and laid flat on its back with the head encased in an irregular lump of clay. With infinite care David begins to carve. Half-an-hour goes by, and there is now a knight in armour with his hands folded across his chest. David had visited a cathedral with his father, and the knight, guarding his tomb, fired the boy's imagination. For the moment his vision of the knight and the clay beneath his fingers constitute his world, and there is complete harmony between them.

Ricki is rarely still, and his restless energy is a symptom of tension. His father was killed in a car accident, and his mother is now running the business single-handed, working flat out. Ricki is deeply affected by her tension and unhappiness, and he suffers from acute anxiety and is easily upset. Although he is a pleasant little boy he makes few friends because he is impatient and finds difficulty in settling down to a game or job for long enough to finish it. Ricki's father played the violin and in his spare time made violins and violas. The boy had spent hours listening to his father play and loved to hear orchestral music, and although he can no longer share this experience with his father the music still holds him. In service time his tensions fall away and he sits completely still as he listens to the recorded orchestral music. For at least a few minutes Ricki's conflicts are forgotten, and he and the music are one.

Such experiences of integration we describe in a number of

ways. We say, 'I was completely caught up', 'I lost all sense of time', 'I forgot where I was', or 'I forgot myself altogether'. We express an experience of our single self, and such expressions contrast sharply with those which show that we are well aware of the existence of conflicting selves leading to disequilibrium: 'I was beside myself', 'I'm in two minds about it', 'You must forgive me. I'm not myself'. The feeling of being torn apart by conflicting selves is all too familiar. It destroys efficiency, and we become incapable of using our faculties to the full. Inner direction becomes impossible because we lack singleness of purpose and we are at the mercy of any other direction which comes along. It is only when all that goes into making life is unified within the person that one can truly be said to live.

19

Helping children to live

From the moment of his birth the child's main concern is to make himself a person, to create his own personality. Education is of use to him only in as far as it helps to further this aim.

The process of becoming is the process of learning, and learning how to become a person is what life is about. During his early years the child experiences life directly, not at an intellectual distance but as an immediate reality; it is only experience which develops in him a conceptual view of his world.

What the teacher does for the child must fit in with what the child is trying to do for himself. The only way to help the child in this job is by giving him access to a wealth of reality, because this is the only material he knows how to use.

The teacher is expected to do her job within the bounds of a classroom, and this situation presents her with a major problem which few teachers overcome successfully; namely, that of restricting the child to a unit of space which tends to become divorced from the real world beyond the confines of the school.

The child's most important contact with reality in any classroom is through the personality of the teacher herself. What she is remains his most powerful aid to learning, and he depends on her for what he can experience of the world beyond the classroom walls.

The teacher of young children knows that words are not her most effective means of conveying impressions of the world to the child. Until many years of experience have provided words with meaning they can convey little more than pale images of reality. In her anxiety to remedy their inadequacy the teacher resorts to the use of teaching aids. Unfortunately these aids are easier to procure and to use than real objects, and they tend to be regarded as a means of teaching in themselves. The teacher forgets that they are only substitutes.

A child brought up in the Seychelle Islands has coconuts for playthings, and he writes of them like this: 'The coconuts in Seychelles were the biggest in the world. They were called coco-de-mer. I couldn't hold one because they were too big and too heavy. They used them to make fruit bowls. They made them by taking the husk off and then splitting it in half. They ate the jelly and coconut and just had the shell split open. They varnished the inside and outside. Then the fruit bowl was made. They were called coco-de-mer as the first ones had been washed up from the sea. There were ordinary coconuts as well, they only made little things out of those because they were meant for eating. The small coconuts are about six inches high and eight inches wide.'

This child's impressions are sound because he has handled the real object. Not even a film would convey impressions as vivid as these, and the still pictures, photographs or diagrams which children are so often shown convey very little live information at all.

There is no adequate substitute for reality. Whenever it is possible we should put into the hands of children real objects and let them teach him what he is capable of learning from them. The teacher cannot, of course, persuade the Amazon to flow through the playground or bring London Bridge into the classroom, and in this kind of situation she must resort to representation. Even so, the symbol can only convey its message about reality if there is some experience in the life of the child to which it can be attached. However small the scrap of reality may be, we give the child something to touch, hear and enjoy at first hand; and then we can extend his experience with the aid of symbols.

Perception on the part of the child results in images, and his sensations provide him with feelings. His discovery of reality is a synthesis of images and feelings. Activities are educative only if they reproduce faithfully the conditions of real life, and this is the meaning of imaginative education.

What exactly does learning from reality involve? It means accepting the whole of life, the heights and the depths, the rough with the smooth. Protecting the child from certain aspects of life will make him unable to deal with the whole of it, and parts of his personal adjustment will never take place.

So afraid have parents and teachers become of the word 'insecurity' that they remove all that threatens the child and strive to secure for him a completely happy childhood. While happiness and security are confidence-builders and help to ensure the mental health of an individual, there may be a danger in making a child too happy. Happiness is not in itself a goal, it is only a by-product of satisfactory living, and how do we recognise it unless we have been deprived of it? A completely happy child would have little on which to base sympathy and understanding of those less fortunate than himself.

Positive living is the reverse side of a coin. The person who is capable of inspirational activity must accept the trough of depression as its partner. Capacity to feel intensely brings sorrow as well as joy, frustration as well as satisfaction and hate as well as love. The education of the whole man implies full personal involvement in the constant struggle to maintain equilibrium between the extremities which are the laws of life.

Within the safe protection of loving parents and teachers children can experience frustration and disappointment, distress and failure, and learn how to regard these experiences not as enemies to his personality but as essential forms of

129

stimulation, without which personality would remain inadequate. They will learn, too, that no experience lasts for ever and that by facing up to a difficult problem they are halfway to solving it.

Parents and teachers are often in a position to protect the child from that which threatens his happiness. In the name of love they may protect him and divert the danger or solve his problem for him. It takes love of a very high order to stand by and, as one parent expressed it, 'let them learn for themselves. Well, perhaps you don't exactly watch them go over the precipice, but you let them come near enough to know what it's like beyond.'

If life is to mean anything at all to a child, he must have access to the full range of its experiences. Only then can he be said to live and to have the opportunity for full development of his personality.

Appendix 1

REFERENCE MATERIAL

A. Books for Background Reading

Allport, Gordon W. *Pattern and Growth in Personality.* New York and London: Holt, Rinehart and Winston, 1961.

Dimmack, Max. *Modern Art Education in the Primary School.* Macmillan, 1959.

Hadfield, John. *A Book of Beauty: an anthology of words and pictures.* Edward Hutton, 1958.

Jeffreys, M. V. C. *Personal Values in the Modern World.* Penguin, 1962.

Lowenfeld, Viktor and Brittain, W. Lambert. *Creative and Mental Growth.* London: Collier-Macmillan, 1964.

Marshall, Sybil. *An Experiment in Education.* C.U.P, 1963.

Marshall, Sybil. *Adventure in Creative Education.* Pergamon, 1968.

Read, Sir Herbert. *Education through Art.* Faber, 1958.

Read, Sir Herbert. (Ed.) *This Way Delight.* Faber, 1957.

Robertson, Seonaid. *Creative Crafts in Education.* Routledge, 1952.

Robertson, Seonaid. *Crafts and Contemporary Culture.* Harrap.

B. Books for Reference

Buckels, Constance and Alec. *The Little Scissors Man.* Macmillan, 1959.

Creative Play Series. Batsford.

Early, Mabel. *Creative Crafts for Children.* Batsford.

Green, Peter. *Creative Print Making.* Batsford, 1964.

Hartung, Rolf. *Creative Corrugated Paper Craft.* Batsford, 1966.

Hils, Karl. *Creative Crafts.* Batsford, 1966.

Johnson, Pauline. *Creating with Paper.* Edward Ward and Nicholas Kaye, 1960.

Maile, Anne. *Tie-and-Dye as a Present-Day Craft.* Mills and Boon, 1963.

Marks, Winnifred. *Lively Drawing with Pencil and Brush.* Books 1-4. Macmillan, 1946.

Meyers, Hans. *150 Techniques in Art.* Batsford, 1963.

Meyers, Hans. *150 Themes in Art.* Batsford. 1965.

Proud, Norah. *Textile Printing and Dyeing.* Batsford, 1965.

Röttger, Ernst. *Creative Paper Craft.* Batsford, 1961.

Röttger, Ernst. *Creative Wood Craft.* Batsford, 1961.

Röttger, Ernst. *Creative Clay Craft.* Batsford, 1963.

Rottger, Ernst and Klante, Deiter. *Creative Drawing: Point and Line.* Batsford, 1964.

Tritten, Gottfried. *Art Techniques for Children (Primary and Secondary).* Batsford, 1964.

Wilcox, Joy. *Printed Rag Toys.* Batsford, 1967.

C. Books on Home-made Musical Instruments

Blocksidge, K. *Making Musical Apparatus and Instruments.* Nursery School Association, 1962.

Galloway, M. *Making and Playing Bamboo Pipes.* Dryad Press, 1967.

Roberts, R. *Musical Instruments Made to be Played.* Dryad Press, 1965.

D. Firms Supplying Materials

General

Dryad Handicrafts, Northgates, Leicester
Winsor and Newton, Wealdstone, Harrow, Middx.
Reeves and Sons Ltd., Lincoln Rd., Enfield, Middx.
Rowney, 10/11 Percy St., London W.1

Papers for all Purposes

Hunt and Broadhurst, Botley Rd., Oxford
F. G. Kettle and Co., 23 New Oxford St., W.C.1

T. N. Lawrence, Bleeding Heart Yard, Greville St., E.C.1 (An excellent range of hand-made papers.)

CLAY

Potglaze Ltd., Whant House, Copeland St., Stoke-on-Trent (Clay and prepared bodies.)

Pike Bros., Poole, Dorset (Off-white Bull Clay.)

Wengers Ltd., Etruria, Stoke-on-Trent

Acme Marls Ltd., Clough St., Hanley, Stoke-on-Trent

PAINT

James Beard, Great Ancoats St., Manchester (Poster paint in bulk.)

Margros Poster Paint, Tannery House, Tannery Lane, Send, Woking, Surrey

MISCELLANEOUS

Brushes: Teme Valley Brush Co., Indigo St., Teme Valley Trading Estate, Newcastle, 11

Powder inks in 9d. drums: Brusho Inks, J. B. Duckett & Co., Sheffield

Ball-point Colour Tubes: Tui Chim, Sepea Developments Ltd., 89 Oxford St., Manchester 1

Appendix 2

THE RELIGIOUS EDUCATION OF YOUNG CHILDREN:
SOME USEFUL BOOKS
Compiled by Robin Protheroe

In choosing books for the children's own reference, it is helpful to bear in mind some general principles:

1. Miracles are likely to be misunderstood as magic in the intuitive and concrete-operational stages of thinking.
2. At these stages children will not be able to deduce from parables abstract truths about God or general principles of behaviour, even with the help of the teacher.

3. There is great danger in so stressing the divinity of Jesus that he ceases to be regarded as a real man.
4. Many Old Testament stories which may be familiar to the teacher should be avoided, because they express pre-Christian religious concepts which will confuse the child until he is able to read and understand them in their historical context.

For children of 5-7 years
Stories about Jesus are best introduced as part of a 'life-theme', e.g. 'Homes': Jesus' home and family, the synagogue school, the carpenter's shop. A few parables may be introduced as stories without dealing with the meaning of the parable e.g. 'The Sower', 'The Good Samaritan', 'The House on the Rock'.

Recommended books

Friends of Jesus	Betty Smith	Lutterworth
Jesus the Friend	Ladybird	Wills and Hepworth
Jesus the Helper	Ladybird	Wills and Hepworth
The Good Samaritan	Arch Books	Concordia
The House on the Rock	Arch Books	Concordia

The *Dove* books (Chapmans) are a beautifully illustrated series but, apart from 'Zacchaeus the Publican', the text is usually too difficult for young children. They are more useful if the teacher retells the story and simply shows the pictures.

The Christmas Story: There are innumerable books for children on this theme, but teachers should read the text very carefully. One good example is *The Christmas Story* by R. Herrmann (Macmillan).

For children of 7-11 years
Again many of the stories may well be introduced as part of a 'life-theme', but with older juniors a more systematic

study will be possible. The emphasis will still be on Jesus as a man, and more background information can be given so that he is seen in his historical and geographical context. Although much of the life and teaching of Jesus is beyond the grasp of a child in the Primary School, valuable work can be done in giving a vivid picture of life in Palestine at the time of Jesus and in Israel today, and this will make teaching at secondary level significant. There are many books on this subject, of which the following are particularly good:

The Land Where Jesus Lived. G. C. Mabbutt and J. L. Holm. Schofield Sims.

Susan and the Land of the Bible. S. Gillsater. Heinemann.

This is Israel. M. Sasek. W. H. Allen.

Let's Travel in the Holy Land. Darel Geis. Odhams.

The Palestine of Jesus. B. R. Youngman. Hulton Press.

This is a secondary textbook, but is useful for pictures.

The following are recommended for the teacher's reference:

Everyday Life in Old Testament Times. E. W. Heaton. Batsford.

Everyday Life in New Testament Times. A. C. Bouquet. Batsford.

Models for the Scripture Lesson. M. Barwell. National Scripture Society Union.

The Historical Jesus. H. Zahrnt. Collins.

For juniors there are few really good textbooks, but the following are sound:

The *Phoenix* Series. J. L. Holm and G. C. Mabbutt. Schofield Sims:

Learning about God, and *Peter, Friend and Follower of Jesus.*

The World's Best Seller.

The Temple, and *Jesus the King.*

Handbook for Teachers. Nat. Soc. and S.P.C.K.

Jesus of Nazareth. Joy Harington. Buckhampton Press.

For older juniors, *New World* books designed for secondary pupils may be helpful:
The Beginning. Alan Dale. Oxford University Press.
The Message. Alan Dale. Oxford University Press.

VISUAL AIDS
The teacher may tell excellent stories about Jesus and yet do untold damage to a child's understanding by illustrating them with bad pictures. For a list of the latest visual aids see:
A Guide to Audio-Visual Aids for Religious Education (5s.) available from:

> National Catechetical Centre,
> 13-15 Denbigh Road,
> Notting Hill Gate,
> London, W.11.

Some of the La Rochette pictures are useful, but particularly good are the two series on the 'Life of Christ' and 'The Teaching of Christ' by the Benedictine Nuns of Vita et Pax School, Cockfosters, all available from the National Cathechetical Centre.

For older juniors, S.P.C.K. Christian Year Book Pictures, including fine art reproductions in colour, 15″ by 21″, are very good value at 2s. 6d. each. They include:

The Cleansing of the Temple	El Creco.
The Tribute Money	attrib. Titian.
The Entry into Jerusalem	Fra Angelico.

CHILD-CENTRED RELIGIOUS EDUCATION
Teachers who are concerned that their children's religious education should, like other aspects of their education, be firmly rooted in experience, will regard the reading of *Readiness for Religion* by Ronald Goldman (Routledge & Kegan Paul) as of first importance. Rupert Hart-Davis publish *An Infant*

School Teacher's Religious Diary by Freda and Philip Cliff and a 'Readiness for Religion' series of work-cards and workbooks for children, under Dr Goldman's editorship. Also very highly recommended is the series *Alive in God's World* by the Wadderton Group (Church Information Office). These four books (for 5-7's, 7-9's, 9-11's and 11-13's) are intended for use in Anglican Sunday schools and need to be adapted for use in maintained schools, but they are full of excellent suggestions for stories, illustrations and activities of all kinds, and for the worship which may grow from them. The new agreed syllabus of the ILEA, 'Learning for Life' (available from County Hall, S.E.1, price 15s.), offers a complete guide to the religious education of children from their nursery years to adolescence. The information and advice it contains are of outstanding value.

WORSHIP

Margaret Kitson's books, *Infant Praise* and *Infant Prayer* (O.U.P.), can almost be said to be standard works. In addition, the *Morning Cockerel Hymn Book* (Rupert Hart-Davis) and the *Morning Cockerel Book of Readings* (Rupert Hart-Davis) can provide welcome variety. *Praying with Beginners*, by Christopher and Margaret Bacon, and *Praying with Primaries* by Dorothy Wilton (National Christian Educational Council) are recommended, not as sources of 'written prayers', but as suggesting ways in which teachers may wish to help children to compose their own prayers.

Many of the popular 'folk gospel' songs appeal to young children melodically and rhythmically, especially some from *Faith, Folk and Clarity* (Galliard), *Joy is Like the Rain* (Vanguard Music Ltd.), and *The Gospel Song Book* by Sidney Carter (Chapman). A wide selection of modern tunes to familiar hymns, and collections of entirely new hymns in a modern idiom, are published by Josef Weinberger, 33 Cranford St., W.1.

Appendix 3

MUSIC FOR YOUNG CHILDREN:
SOME TWENTIETH CENTURY MUSIC FOR LISTENING
Compiled by Malcolm Anderton

Béla Bartók:
  Concerto for Orchestra
  Pianoforte Concerto No. 3
  Violin Concerto
  Viola Concerto
  Music for Strings, Percussion and Celesta
  Dance Suite for Orchestra

Ernest Bloch:
  'Schelomo' for Cello and Orchestra
  Concerto Grosso for Strings
  Nocturne for Piano, Violin and Cello
  Two interludes from 'Macbeth'
  Symphony 'Israel'

Benjamin Britten:
  Sinfonia da Requiem
  Spring Symphony
  Variations on a Theme by Frank Bridge for Strings
  Four Sea Interludes from 'Peter Grimes'
  The Young Person's Guide to the Orchestra
  Sonata for Cello and Pianoforte
  Serenade for Tenor, Horn and Strings

John Cage:
  Fontana Mix
  Sonatas and Interludes for Prepared Piano

Claude Debussy:
  Prélude à l'après-midi d'un faune
  Three Nocturnes for Orchestra
  La Mer, for Orchestra
  Children's Corner Suite
  Preludes, Books 1 and 2

Frederick Delius:
  English Rhapsody 'Brigg Fair'
  Intermezzo 'The Walk to the Paradise Garden'
  Mass of Life
  Appalachia
  On Hearing the First Cuckoo in Spring
  Dance Rhapsody No. 1
Ernst von Dohnányi:
  Variations on a Nursery Song
Edward Elgar:
  Violin Concerto
  Cello Concerto
  Enigma Variations
  Falstaff
  Introduction and Allegro for Strings
Georges Enesco:
  Roumanian Rhapsody No. 1
Manuel de Falla:
  Three Dances from 'The Three-Cornered Hat'
  Suite for El Senor Brujo
  Nights in the Gardens of Spain
Paul Hindemith:
  Symphony 'Mathis der Maler'
  Concert Music for Brass and Strings
  Symphonic Dances
  Nobilissima Visione
  The Swanturner
Arthur Honegger:
  Concertino for Pianoforte and Orchestra
  King David
  Symphony No. 3
Jacques Ibert:
  Divertimento
  'Escales'

John Ireland:
    A London Overture
    Piano Concerto
    These Things Shall Be
    Piano Pieces

Dmitri Kabalersky:
    Violin Concerto

Aram Khachaturian:
    Piano Concerto

Zoltan Kodaly:
    Concerto for Orchestra
    Suite from 'Háry János'
    Dances from 'Galanta'
    Dances from 'Marosszék'
    Variations on the Peacock

Gustav Mahler:
    Song of the Earth

Darius Milhaud:
    Suite Provençale

Sergé Prokofiev:
    Classical Symphony
    Symphony No. 5
    Peter and the Wolf
    Lieutenant Kije
    Ballet Suite 'Romeo and Juliet'
    Violin Concerto No. 2

Sergei Rachmaninov:
    Symphony No. 2
    Piano Concerto Nos. 1, 2, 3
    Rhapsody on a theme of Paganini
    Songs

Maurice Ravel:
    Piano Concerto
    Concerto for the Left Hand

Pavane for a Dead Infanta
String Quartet

Arnold Schoenberg:
Five Pieces for Orchestra
Pierrot Lunaire

Igor Stravinsky:
Firebird Suite
Rite of Spring
Petroushka
Symphony of Psalms
Mass
A Soldier's Tale

Ralph Vaughan Williams:
London Symphony
Sea Symphony
Overture and March 'The Wasps'
Fantasia on a Theme of Thomas Tallis
Job
Serenade to Music

William Walton:
Viola Concerto
Overture 'Portsmouth Point'
Façade
Belshazzar's Feast
Symphonies Nos. 1 and 2

The above suggestions are intended as starting points for the exploration of these and other composers. Much that children can enjoy has been written by composers such as Bliss, Respighi, Dallapiccola, Messiaen, Roussel, Sibelius, Richard Strauss, Wolf-Ferrari, Tippett, Copland, Bacher, Xenakis, Berio, Chavez, Lutoslawski, Pendereki, Harrison Birtwistle, Alexander Goehr, Peter Maxwell Davies, Stockhausen and Ives.

Index